FLIGHT HANDBOOK OF MARKETING KNOWLEDGE

How to Implement the
Flight School Marketing System
In Your Flight School Business to
Enroll More Students and Train More Pilots

Written by Tim Jedrek
Edited by Dr. Dianyi Liu
First Edition

RIGHT RUDDER MARKETING

The author and publisher shall in no event be held liable to any party for any damages arising directly or indirectly from the use of this material. Every effort has been made to accurately represent this information and there is no guarantee that you will earn any money using any of these techniques.

While the publisher has made every effort to verify the information here, neither the author nor publisher assumes any responsibility for errors in, omissions from, or different interpretation of the subject matter. This information may be subject to varying laws and practices in different areas, states, countries. The reader assumes responsibility for use of this information.

This publication is licensed to the individual reader only. Duplication or distribution by any other means including email, photocopying, and video recording to a person other than the original purchaser is a violation of international copyright law.

Published by Right Rudder Marketing LLC
Copyright © 2024 Right Rudder Marketing LLC
All rights reserved
ISBN - 9798338151310

Dedication

This book is dedicated to all of the flight school owners and pilots that work hundreds of hours of overtime each month to train more pilots.

The love of aviation brings us all together. I hope that this book will amplify your passion for aviation and help the aviation industry as a whole by enrolling and training more students to serve the ever increasing demand for pilots.

I'm dedicating this book to YOU, so you can grow your flight school business faster than ever before.

Acknowledgments

I'd like to acknowledge all of the flight school businesses that have allowed us to help them with the task of growing their online presence over the past few years. On behalf of my team, we are honored to work with such great people and we hope for continued success and growth.

In addition, this book is based on real world case studies of flight school businesses across the country that doubled, tripled, and 10X'd their leads and student pilot enrollments by getting their internet marketing done right.

I'd like to acknowledge our flight school partners for allowing us to use their stories as the foundation of this book.

I would be remiss if I did not mention my loving family that has been with me since day one. My lovely and endearing wife, Dianyi, helped proofread and edit this book. She's supported me as I worked countless hours to grow the Right Rudder Marketing business.

And lastly my father, Tonie. My dad bought me a discovery flight more than five years ago. Without that initial spark, I would have never had the opportunity or the idea to become a pilot and serve the aviation community.

A Quick Note

Here at Right Rudder Marketing, our goal is to help educate flight school owners like yourself about the world of digital marketing. Head on over to our website rightruddermarketing.com to check out tons of free education content, training guides, and videos.

We release monthly webinars on new marketing topics and we have featured guest speakers on our weekly podcast. If you haven't checked that out yet, please follow us on social media.

Got questions on the content of this book? Contact us. Send an email, give us a call, or simply shoot us a message. Our goal is to be a supportive resource for YOU.

1-314-804-1200
info@rightruddermarketing.com
https://rightruddermarketing.com/schedule-call

Table of Contents

Introduction

Chapter 1. The Flight School Marketing System

Chapter 2. Marketing 101

Chapter 3. Prospective Student Pilot Leads from Your Website

Chapter 4. Search Engine Optimization Hacks

Chapter 5. Ranking Top on Google Maps and Search

Chapter 6. Social Media Marketing

Chapter 7. Email Marketing for Flight Schools

Chapter 8. Advertising Online with Pay Per Click

Chapter 9. Track Progress and Automate Tasks

Chapter 10. Create Your Flight School Marketing System

References

Additional Resources

Introduction

In this book we're going to be talking about how you can double and even triple your student pilot enrollments by getting your internet marketing done right in your flight school business.

I'm super excited to see you here, because if you're reading this it shows that you're interested in growing your business and leveraging the internet to the fullest extent possible.

I can't wait to share with you what we've learned here at Right Rudder Marketing working with flight schools all across the country to do their digital marketing.

Let me emphasize that this book is based on case studies and real life examples.

This isn't me yanking your chain or throwing you some buzz words and hypothetical trends. It's truly based on the flight schools that we've helped to double, triple, and in some cases 10X their student enrollments and revenue.

It's good solid information that you can sink your teeth into and feel confident that if done correctly, will have an impact on the growth of your flight school.

We've been able to accomplish this for many of our flight schools in a short time frame by implementing what we call the Flight School Marketing System. This book is all about how you can create your very own Flight School Marketing System in your own business.

What Would It Be Like If?...

Here's a quick question for you. Have you ever wondered what would it be like:

- To have a dominant presence in your local area and airport that positions you as the top flight school that new students should be calling?
- To have a continuous flow of prospective students and high quality leads calling into your business that find you purely through the internet?
- To know that you were leveraging the internet to its fullest potential in terms of exposure, leads, and profits?
- To have new challenges of expanding your business to new locations and airports, buying new aircraft, and hiring more team members and instructors?

These are the things that I want for you through this book. I want you to accomplish your goals and train more pilots.

What You'll Find in This Book

As you read this book, here's what you'll learn:

- Our three step framework of the Flight School Marketing System that covers the most important aspects of marketing your flight school online.
- How you can get your flight school ranked on the first page for the most important keywords in your area.
- A proven strategy for getting ranking on the Google Map listings in your market.
- How to create a pay per click advertising campaign that can be scaled for nonstop lead generation.

Who Am I?

Before we get too deep, I'd like to introduce myself. Who am I and why should you even bother listening to what I have to say?

My name is Tim Jedrek. I'm the owner and founder of Right Rudder Marketing. I had over a decade of experience working in corporate food manufacturing and quality assurance management before obtaining my private pilot certificate. It was a great career and one that helped fund my pilot certificate.

I started at the bottom as an entry level technician and worked my way up the ladder to the department head as a quality manager. I am very proud of the teams I managed and the work we completed. However, I always had an itch. I had "the aviation bug." After I did my intro discovery flight, I knew I had to be in aviation.

Part time, I built websites and programmed software as my side gig. In an effort to grow my clients' businesses, I dived head first into marketing and sales. I attended conferences, read books, took courses to further my skills, and found mentors and coaches to guide me on the path of success.

Later on, I combined my passions of growing businesses, software engineering, and flying into a new company called

Right Rudder Marketing where we help flight schools grow and scale their businesses by enrolling more student pilots.

This led to the development of the Flight School Marketing System which I've created specifically for flight school owners. We've been able to help flight schools go from virtually non-existent to now where they're the dominant flight school in their market and airport.

Being the founder of Right Rudder Marketing has also afforded me the opportunity to speak at multiple venues and sponsor aviation communities and events like NAFI (National Association of Flight Instructors), FSANA (Flight School Association of North America), and King Schools.

My passion is helping flight schools grow so everything I'm going to mention in the following chapters is based on real world experience and knowledge you can take to the bank.

What We Do

This brings me to talk a little bit about my marketing agency, Right Rudder Marketing. Yes, we specialize in working with flight schools to help them take their internet marketing to the next level with a custom built Flight School Marketing System.

We set up your website, ensure it's optimized for the search engines, write your content, manage your blog, manage ad campaigns, set up CRMs, and develop your authority and reputation online.

Our team is based in St. Louis, MO. We are a team of account managers, writers, SEO specialists, graphic designers, web developers, and pilots.

Working With You

We'd love the opportunity to work with you and implement the Flight School Marketing System for you. But that's not what the purpose of this book is. This isn't a sales presentation.

My goal is to provide you with our specific strategies and knowledge I have on how to market your flight school business online.

It's just pure value and content because I want to give you our best knowledge and information on how to proactively market your flight school business on your own.

If you were to take this information and implement it, I'd want for you to be able to succeed with it.

Sure we'd love to work with you. We'd love to have you as a flight school partner and client. But let's finish our pre-flight and walk around first.

Let's learn the marketing fundamentals and strategies we employ to grow flight school businesses. And if you want to reach out and give us a call, I'll be here on the other side waiting to say hello.

-Tim Jedrek

1-314-804-1200
info@rightruddermarketing.com
https://rightruddermarketing.com/schedule-call

The Flight School Marketing System

Chapter 1

The purpose of implementing the Flight School Marketing System in your business is to achieve business growth, scale, and impact. This book will provide you with the marketing procedures that we've used and seen success with and how our team at Right Rudder Marketing implemented the Flight School Marketing System.

Figure 1-1. The three outcomes of implementing the Flight School Marketing System

In essence, there are three main steps creating your very own Flight School Marketing System. The first step is to bring potential student pilots to your website and social media. The next step is to have these interested people fill out a form on your website or give you a call. At this stage, they effectively become what most business owners and marketers refer to as leads. The last and final step is converting these leads into customers. These customers are student pilots at your flight school that receive training and eventually to become certificated/rated pilots with the training provided at your flight school.

To achieve these steps, we first need to come up with a PLAN because having a PLAN provides a framework/roadmap to success. Failure to plan is simply planning to fail. Let's break down the PLAN for implementing the Flight School Marketing System at your flight school.

Your Marketing Plan

Similar to how an airplane has different control surfaces, your marketing plan needs to have a variety of different channels and media to reach your target student pilots. Below in *Figure 1-2* is a visual representation of what I call the "Flight School Marketing System." It outlines the approach we use online to drive more interested students to your flight school.

From the top left, we start with your flight school website. Your website is the foundation to your marketing strategy because all of the potential students are going to browse and compare pilot schools using the websites. Your website needs to be set up in such a way that you are able to extract your visitor's contact information so you can start the sales process and have them receive training at your flight school.

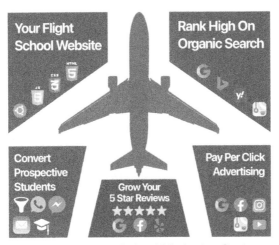

Figure 1-2. Flight School Marketing System

Figure 1-2 moving clockwise, you have ranking high on organic search. What this means is having your website ranked high on Google and other search engines. This is accomplished in a multitude of ways through what is called SEO (search engine optimization) - a topic in which we'll take a deep dive later in chapters 4 and 5.

In the bottom right corner, you have pay per click advertising which is advertising on the internet. There are different platforms most popularly Google and Meta. This is where you pay to get in front of your target audience online.

At the very bottom on heading 180, we have growing your five star reviews. This gets into reputation management and how your flight school and your brand is being portrayed online. We need to make a concerted effort to continue to grow our reviews online so that we can establish our flight school as the authority in our local area.

Lastly, in the bottom left corner we have converted prospective students into enrolled students that continue their training at your flight school. We need to approach enrollments at our flight schools as a sales process. We need to qualify our prospective students and lead them forward in our process all the way through onboarding and retention.

At first glance, considering all the marketing options available in the Flight School Marketing System might be overwhelming. However, to maximize your lead flow from the internet, you need to develop a plan which covers each of these online marketing opportunities. The purpose of this book is to outline a plan that will transform you from an online marketing newbie to the dominant player in your area. Your flight school will be **the #1 flight school** in your local area.

Throughout this book, we lay the foundation to:
- Map out your online marketing plan (Website, SEO, PPC, social media, CRM, automation, etc.) and develop your Flight School Marketing System
- Start with the marketing fundamentals (Market, Message, Medium) before jumping headfirst into developing your Flight School Marketing System
- Set up your website and get your business online
- Understand Mobile Optimization for mobile visitors
- Understand Website Conversion Fundamentals to ensure that your website converts visitors into leads
- Understand how search engines work and the differences between the paid, organic, and map listings
- Optimize with Search Engine Optimization:
    - How to conduct keyword research
    - What are the most commonly searched keywords in the pilot training industry

- How to achieve the maximum result by mapping out the pages on your website
- How to optimize your website for ranking
- How to improve your website's visibility
- How to enhance rankings
- How to generate content to receive attention from student pilots
- Optimize Google Maps:
  - What is Google Maps ranking (NAP, Citations, Consistency and Reviews)
  - How to establish a strong name, address, and phone number profile
  - How to properly claim and optimize your Google My Business Local Listing
  - How to develop authority for your map listing via citation development
  - What are the top citation sources for your flight school
  - How to get five star reviews from your customers and students
- Utilize social media marketing (Facebook, Instagram, Twitter, LinkedIn and other social platforms)
- Create Content to tap into the power of YouTube and other video sharing websites to enhance your visibility and drive better conversions
- Use Pay Per Click Marketing (Google Ads, Bing Search, Meta Facebook and Instagram) to maximize the profitability of your Pay Per Click Marketing efforts
  - Why PPC should be part of your overall online marketing strategy
  - Why most PPC campaigns fail
  - What is the Google Ads Auction process

- How to configure and manage your Pay Per Click campaign for maximum ROI
- Track, Measure, and Quantify to ensure your investment is generating a strong return
- Leverage email marketing tools (Constant Contact, Mail Chimp, etc.) to connect with your customers on a deeper level, receive more reviews, get more social media connections, and ultimately get repetitive referral business.

When it comes to digital marketing for your flight school, we briefly touched on the various internet marketing channels that are available. We'll dive a little deeper into each marketing channel below.

Search Engine Optimization

Search Engine Optimization (SEO) is the process of increasing your company's visibility on major search engines (Google, Yahoo, Bing, etc.) in the organic, non-paid listings as consumers are searching for your products or services.

When you do a search on Google or any other search engine, you'll see that there are different components that are displayed to you when you look at the search results. These are:

- **Paid Listings** - The area along the top and side that advertisers can bid on and pay for in order to obtain decent placement in the search engines.
- **Organic Listings** – The area in the body of the Search Engine Results page
- **Map Listings** – These are the listings which come up beneath the paid listings and above the organic listings in a number of searches

Search Engine Optimization involves getting your website to show up in the Organic and Map Listings. These listings will account for a majority of the traffic that will come to your website.

By strategically structuring your website's content, structure, and meta information, you can improve its ranking in organic, non-paid search results. This, in turn, ensures that your aviation and flight school services are more easily discoverable by prospective students actively seeking information relevant to pilot training.

As search algorithms evolve and update, staying ahead in the online marketplace becomes essential. We're going to get into the specifics of SEO and look at a few strategies tailored specifically for aviation businesses and flight schools. This book will provide you with actionable insights and help you develop your very own Flight School Marketing System.

Search Engine Marketing / Pay Per Click

Search Engine Marketing (SEM) or PPC (Pay Per Click) is using Google's and Bing's paid programs where you purchase and buy top positions on their search platforms.

There are three really important benefits of PPC:
1. Your keyword listings will appear on search engines almost immediately
2. You only have to pay when someone actually clicks on your listing – hence the term Pay Per Click Marketing
3. You can get your ads to show up on national keyword terms in the areas/cities in which your flight school is based out of (think keywords like *"how to be a pilot"*)

PPC Marketing works on an auction system similar to that of eBay. You simply choose your keywords and propose a bid of what you would be willing to pay for each click.

Using Pay Per Click advertising is a great way to get your company's website to appear at the top of the search engines right away, driving qualified traffic to your website.

Social Media Marketing

Social media has changed the way humans think and communicate with one another. It's a modern phenomena that has restructured our relationships with one another. Social media is also one of the primary places on the internet where people spend the majority of their time.

So if your ideal customers and your future student pilots are spending their time on social media, why wouldn't you invest the resources to reach them. Just take a look at some the staggering statistics on Facebook:

- Facebook had **2.989 billion monthly active users** in April 2023 placing it 1st in the ranking of the world's most 'active' social media platforms[3]
- American users spend on average 33 minutes per day on Facebook. Facebook was the platform with the largest amount of time spent daily.[4] For mobile users, the average time spent on the app is **57 minutes** daily[5]
- 71.43% of the American population are on Facebook. There is an estimated **239 million Americans** that have an account on Facebook[6]

Facebook is not the only social media platform out there. Many of your future students are also on Instagram, YouTube, TikTok, Twitter, and LinkedIn. The best approach to marketing your business on social media is to leverage all of these platforms to reach your students and consistently post content and interact with all of your customers.

Use social media platforms to connect with your immediate social circle, your past customers, and your new customers. By doing so, you can solidify and maintain existing relationships, remain in the minds of your customers, and ultimately increase repeat and referral business.

The most important part of utilizing social media for your flight school business is that you are developing and then nurturing an online community centered around your flight school. You are creating the connections and the platform for your students to interact with you and your flight school business as well as their fellow peers and classmates.

Video Marketing

Did you know YouTube is the second most used search engine on the market?[7] Would you guess it is even ahead of Bing and Yahoo? It's true! Millions of people conduct YouTube searches on a daily basis. In fact, in 2020 Youtube was the most visited site on the internet.[8] Most business owners are so focused on SEO and PPC that they completely neglect the opportunities that video and YouTube provide.

Incorporating a Video Marketing Strategy into your business approach can prove to be a game changer. Beyond the confines of conventional SEO, video content offers a unique avenue to bolster your online presence. Imagine not only being discoverable through text based searches but also through engaging visual content that captures the attention of your target audience. This strategic integration not only grants you additional visibility in search results for your chosen keywords but also acts as a dynamic supplement to your broader SEO initiatives.

Furthermore, the impact of a well crafted Video Marketing Strategy extends beyond mere visibility. It can significantly enhance the overall effectiveness of your SEO efforts by diversifying the types of content associated with your brand. The dynamic nature of video content allows you to connect with your audience on a more human level, fostering a deeper engagement that transcends traditional text based approaches.

Moreover, the incorporation of videos into your online presence has the potential to improve visitor conversion rates. Visual content has a unique ability to convey complex information in a digestible and compelling manner, making it a powerful tool to influence and persuade your audience. By leveraging the captivating nature of videos, you can create a more immersive and memorable brand experience, ultimately increasing the likelihood of turning visitors into valued customers.

Making videos for your flight school business doesn't have to be hard. You don't need a studio setup or expensive equipment to get started. In the old days, maybe yes. To create videos, you would need to hire professional videographers, have fancy cameras and software, and spend tons of money and time to create great video content.

But now we have all of those things, which would have cost tens of thousands of dollars back then, in a simple package in our pockets. Our cell phones. Now anyone can create video content using cell phones.

In the upcoming chapters, we delve into the intricacies of Video Marketing Strategies, offering insights, tips, and actionable steps to empower your business in harnessing the full potential of YouTube and video content. Explore how this often overlooked component of digital marketing can help drive your online success and increase visibility, engagement, and conversion with your future student pilots.

By implementing a Video Marketing Strategy for your business, you can get additional placement in search results for your keywords, enhance the effectiveness of your SEO efforts and improve visitor conversion.

Email Marketing

Similar to Social Media Marketing, email marketing is a great way to remain present in the minds of your customers and increase repeat business and referrals. Compared to direct mail and newsletters, email marketing is by far the most cost effective means to communicate with your customers.

Picture this: Automated email sequences that are sent to your prospects and customers that are strategically designed to be triggered based on specific customer actions or milestones. This could range from welcoming new prospects when they complete a form on your website, a flight school newsletter, sending personalized updates on upcoming aviation classes, or even celebrating anniversaries of their engagement with your services. By automating these touchpoints, you not only save valuable time but also ensure that your customers receive relevant and timely information, fostering a more personalized and engaging experience.

As we will discuss in the Email Marketing for Flight Schools chapter, we will show how email marketing can be used to effectively draw your customers into your world. Much like following a well thought out flight plan, email automation allows you to streamline and personalize your communication strategy with customers.

Where to Start?

With such a large amount of internet marketing channels, where should you start? I firmly believe that over time, you should be incorporating each of these online marketing strategies into your Flight School Marketing System. Just like when you're doing your run up and you double check to see if all of your flight control surfaces are free and correct, you need to incorporate all of the digital marketing "control surfaces" into your Flight School Marketing System.

However, you must first begin with the foundation - your website and ranking on search engines by listing your website and business on various directories (especially Google My Business) and social media platforms.

You should start looking at the various paid marketing opportunities when your website is set up correctly, ranking on search engines for your most important keywords in the organic, non-paid listings and you are actively engaging in social media activity.

We have found that the biggest and most impactful opportunity is getting ranked organically (in the non-paid listings). You may then leverage the additional profits in paid marketing to further supplement your growth. Once you are ranking well organically and things are firing on all cylinders, then you can start to run a well managed Pay Per Click advertising campaign

I'm very excited to take you on this journey of developing your own Flight School Marketing System. The next chapter is going to be all about understanding the fundamentals of marketing. We will dive into the psychology and nuances of marketing. Once we understand the core concepts of how to influence customer behavior through marketing, we can develop specific strategies in the Flight School Marketing System's "control surfaces" - how to structure your website, how to rank high on search, how to run an effective advertising campaign, how to create videos to dynamically enhance your online presence, and how to communicate with your leads and prospects to get them in the door of your fight school to start their pilot training.

Key Takeaways from Chapter 1

- Focus your flight school business on growth, scale, and impact.
- A successful marketing strategy focuses on making your flight school known, differentiating yourself from other schools, and providing platforms for potential student pilots to reach you.
- There is no one silver bullet that can get your business to become #1. A multi faceted approach is required and you must incorporate various marketing channels to become known in your local area.

> There is no one silver bullet that can get your business to become #1. A multi faceted approach is required and you must incorporate various marketing channels to become known in your local area.

Marketing 101

Chapter 2

Before we get into the nitty gritty of websites, SEO, PPC, etc., we need to make sure that we have a strong foundation of the marketing fundamentals. I talk to flight school owners daily about how to grow their flight schools and they always tend to skip straight past the basic fundamentals and go headfirst into marketing tactics like PPC advertising and social media.

Robert, a flight school owner I was talking to a few months back, had asked for my advice to help his flight school business. "I have a limited budget and I want to decide on upgrading my website or running Facebook ads."

It's a very common question that I always get. "Should we be spending our money on X vs Y?" I'll get asked something like, "I really like the website I made, but it's not getting ranked. What are your tips on SEO and how do I get my website to rank higher?"

My answer to that is that we need to take a quick step back and look at what goals we are trying to accomplish and how our marketing strategy fits these goals.

Our goal is simple:

"To train safe and proficient pilots to be successful in their aviation goals while making a profit."

The goals of your flight school business goes beyond looking at the tools we use. The questions that are being asked are the wrong questions. They focus on the *medium* and not the *message* and not the *market*. Marketing your flight school business will need to encompass not just the *medium*, but also the *message* and the *market*.

This is the 3Ms in marketing. They're the concepts that make your flight school business "sticky" like the tape from 3M. Dialing in these three concepts will help your flight school "stick" to your customers' minds.

1. **Market** - This is the "who." This is understanding who your customers are. They're the reason you set up shop and the reason why you go to work everyday.
2. **Message** - This is the "what." This is understanding what your flight school means to your customers. It's the reason that your customers choose you.
3. **Medium** - This is the "how." This is the tools, platforms, channels, and strategies you use to get your *message* to your *market*.

Figure 2-1. The 3Ms to Marketing.
Market, Message, and Medium

If you focus solely on the *medium* or your marketing tactics, you will likely fail regardless of how well selected that *medium* is. With that being said, you need to go back to the fundamentals. Invest the time and energy in figuring out who your *market* is and determining what your *message* is. By doing so, ALL of your choices as far as which *medium* to use will be vastly more effective.

Market

To be successful in marketing your flight school and growing your business, our first step is to define who our ideal customers are. Let's take a few moments to think about the following questions.

- What does my ideal customer look like? What background are they coming from? What hobbies and interests do they have? What are their personalities like? What jobs do they have? Or maybe your business model is based on having an accelerated pilot program (zero to hero) and your ideal customer is someone finishing or just finished high school? How old are your ideal customers?
- Look at your last 25 customers and evaluate who spent the most money and flew the most, and which customers were genuinely pleased with your service. What are the unique characteristics of those good customers? Do they live in a particular area of town? Do they have a higher income level? How did they hear about your flight school?

As you think about the answers to these questions, we're going to delve deeper into the typical flight school students, so we can pave the way for a more targeted and effective marketing strategy.

Let's begin by revisiting the responses to the questions posed earlier. Identify the prevailing professional and educational backgrounds of your current student base. Are people involved in STEM (science, technology, engineering, math) frequent flyers at your flight school? Do you often find individuals with members of their family with backgrounds in military or aviation among your students? Perhaps there's a group of "gear heads" fascinated by the mechanics and engineering aspects of aircraft and engines that are at your school. Or maybe your customers are people with wanderlust, looking to turn their love of travel into a pilot career. By categorizing these backgrounds, you lay the groundwork for a nuanced understanding of your audience.

A simple exercise that can be done is doing a little role play in your head and writing your thoughts on a piece of paper. Imagine that you are at a coffee shop with your "ideal customer". As you smell the aroma of freshly brewed coffee and breakfast pastries, you look your "ideal customer" in the eye.

- How are your ideal customers dressed?
- What body language and demeanor do they have?
- What do you like about them? What don't you like about them?
- Why do you want to help them?

Your "ideal customer" says that they found out about your flight school and they're thinking about becoming a pilot. They want to know more information about training to be a pilot and they're looking at flight schools in the area. Your "ideal customer" glances back at you and asks, "There's a lot of different flight schools in the area. What makes your flight school different from the others? What do I need to do to get started and train to be a pilot at your flight school? Is pilot training right for me?"

- How do you respond to that?
- What distinguishes your flight school from other flight schools?
- Why should your "ideal customer" choose to start flight training instead of pursuing other things like boating or medical school?

What we just touched on there is your *message*. The answers to those questions make up the *message* you're going to give to your market. We'll get into your *message* more in depth in the upcoming section.

What's important to note is that each flight school's answers will vary slightly because each flight school has a different market.

Some flight schools have a target market of more affluent communities. These flight schools might invest in newer aircraft with upgraded panels and glass cockpits. Whether it's a Cessna or Piper from the 21st century, or maybe they might be partnering with Cirrus Aircraft and only train in fleets of more expensive aircraft.

Other flight schools might want to make flight training more available to demographic groups with less disposable income. They may have an older fleet, but may prioritize having a family environment and affordable pricing.

Some flight schools might specialize in helicopters, light sport, seaplanes, taildraggers, or accelerated zero to hero programs. It really depends on what you as the business owner has defined as your **market** and who you want to serve.

But at the end of the day, we just need to realize that we can't make everyone happy. You're not pizza.

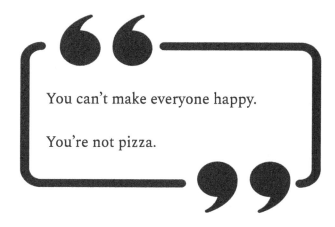

Message

You have to have a unique *message*. This is who you are, what you do, what makes you unique, and why someone should choose your flight school rather than another business offering the same or similar service.

Your competition is not really the other flight schools at your airport or neighboring airports. It's the businesses in the boating industry, the motorcycle and racing industry, horse and equestrian industry, guns, hunting, and camping industry, and other similar industries.

You're also competing with sectors in the marketplace that serve to provide career education and help people change their careers. This can include automotive service technician colleges, law schools, and medical schools.

Basically, any other business that serves to entertain people with their discretionary spend or institutions furthering people's careers and education can be considered a competitor to your flight school business in addition to the other flight schools at your airport.

So what makes you different? Do you still have that piece of paper handy? If not, that's okay. I'll provide the space this time. I really want you to write and participate this time around. It's very important that you take a pen out and write this down. Write down your answer below so you can remember why you're even running a flight school business in the first place.

Why is my flight school unique and different from my competitors?

_____

_____

_____

_____

Great. Glad you wrote that down. This is the *message* that you're going to use in all of your marketing. You've just laid the foundation for a compelling and distinctive message that will set your flight school apart in the competitive landscape. Now, let's explore how to translate these unique qualities into a compelling marketing *message*.

Take a look at the answer you wrote down again. What sets your flight school apart? Is it your personalized approach to training? The state of the art equipment you provide? Perhaps it's the experienced and passionate instructors that make your school stand out. Or is it the environment and community that your flight school offers? Whatever it is, distill these unique elements into a concise and impactful statement. This becomes your Unique Value Proposition (UVP). Your UVP is your powerful message that communicates why potential students should choose your flight school over others. Your UVP is the golden thread that will run through all your marketing *media*. Whether it's a social media post, a Google ad, or a brochure; synthesize your messaging with the distinctive qualities that make your flight school different.

Highlight how your approach aligns with the preferences of your identified ideal customers, creating a narrative that resonates with them on a personal level. Your UVP is the anchor that ties together your marketing efforts forming a cohesive and memorable message.

This then leads into branding. Consistency is the secret ingredient to effective branding. Ensure that your UVP is consistently communicated across all channels. Wherever your prospective student pilots find you, the message should remain cohesive. This not only reinforces your brand identity but also establishes trust and familiarity with potential students. Consistency in messaging breeds confidence, making your flight school the go to choice for individuals seeking aviation training.

The uniqueness that you've identified is the 100LL fuel that will captivate your audience and distinguish your flight school. So, bookmark this page, refer to it often, and let it guide every piece of marketing content you create. You've just set the stage for a powerful and authentic narrative that will resonate with your ideal customers.

My Unique Value Proposition (UVP) is: _____

_____

_____

Medium

Now that we've fleshed out your *message* and your *market*, you can start to think about your *medium*. In order to determine what *medium* will be most effective for you, you need to think about where you can reach your "ideal customer". Where does your "ideal customer" most frequently visit?

Clearly, the Internet is a great *medium* for connecting with your ideal customer who is proactively in the market for your services. Throughout the remainder of this book, we will be explaining the various Internet marketing channels and how you can use them to connect with your ideal customer. Remember, you need to start with the **fundamentals** (message, market and medium) first before running headstrong into any marketing campaign.

Uncovering the "Why?"

The next marketing fundamental we'll cover is the "why". By far this is another business concept that many flight schools gloss over. We assume that just because we love flying, other people will too. We've been in the game for so long, we aviation has become a part of life. We eat, drink, and sleep in aviation. The way we think, the way we process information, has been shaped by our pilot training and we just assume that if we can get a prospective student behind the yoke on a discovery flight that everything will just fall into place.

While I'm not arguing that once we get someone in the cockpit and have them go up in the sky for their first flight, the likelihood of that prospect choosing to start pilot training is high. Flying is pretty cool and it's easy to fall "in love" with aviation.

However, before a prospect even picks up the phone or fills out a form on our website, we need to put ourselves in their shoes and understand why they're even considering flight training. That way, we're able to really refine our **message** for our target **market** using the *media* that our **market** spends most of their time in.

Let's dive into why people choose to start flight training.

To break down any sale ever completed on the face of this earth, the transaction occurred because one party believes that whatever goods or services they are purchasing from the other party will benefit them. What this means is does product or service help me have shelter? Will this product or service help me capture food? Will this product or service help me secure a mate to procreate with?

Looking at those questions above and tying that to flight training, it really just boils down to two fundamental reasons:

1. Sex appeal
2. Resource gathering

Sex Appeal

The FAA Airman statistics published that there were 806,940 pilots registered in the USA in 2023. And of those 806,940 pilots, 82,817 pilots were female[9]. This means that merely 10% of pilots are female and the rest of the population of pilots are overwhelmingly men.

That being said, many people, especially men, choose to pursue pilot training because they want to be "cool" and in turn attract the opposite sex.

It doesn't matter if they're just getting out of high school, middle aged, or nearing retirement. There is an element of wanting to have a higher social status and to stand out amongst their peers and colleagues.

Ever hear the joke about how you can tell if someone is a pilot? The answer is they'll tell you.

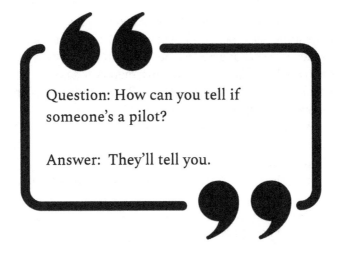

> Question: How can you tell if someone's a pilot?
>
> Answer: They'll tell you.

While it may be just a harmless joke, there is some truth to it. We as pilots have this subconscious urge to tell people that we're pilots. The rationale behind it is that we want them to know our worth. We want them to know our value. At the end of the day, when folks ask a person they've just met, "what do you do for a living?" They are really just using that question as an anchor point to figure out how they themselves compare to the person they're asking.

While some of your student pilots will stop at pursuing pilot training for just merely sex appeal and the "cool" factor, there are many others that will take it a step further and have more personal desires than just becoming attractive to the opposite sex and standing out amongst their peers. These students want to make a career out of aviation.

Resource Gathering

The aviation industry is cyclical yet dynamic. The highly volatile airline pilot demand ebbs and flows depending on the world events, economy, and perceived public opinion on aviation safety.

While there may be time periods where pilot demand is greater than others, flight schools all across the country draw in interested student pilots that have an end goal of making a career in aviation to train in their school every day!

The main driver for that is the perceived opportunity. It's the pot of gold at the end of the rainbow. We would be remiss to say that airline pilots, especially with years of experience and seniority can make a pretty penny.

While pilot salaries are always changing, they are for the most part increasing over time. And although recently there's been some slowdown in hiring at the airlines[10], pilots can still take home multiple six figure salaries depending on their seniority level.

Remember earlier I mentioned how people always ask each other, "what do you do for a living?"

The "what do you do for a living question" also allows people to infer how much money the other person is making and from there, they assess - using money and salary as a measuring tool - how they compare.

Delving further into the topic of money and salaries, money in itself is really just a measure of success that allows a person to exchange their efforts for food, shelter, clothing, and other needs. It's really tied together in a way. The more money a person can make, in tandem their sex appeal will also increase.

Another Resource Sought After

Going away from the money topic for just a bit, another resource I'd like to bring up is time. For the most part, sex appeal and monetary gain are the two main drivers for why people get interested in pilot training. However, there is a certain demographic that pursues flight training for another reason: time.

While not the most common, there are certain people out there in the world that have amassed wealth and in doing so have raised their perceived sexual value, and are more interested in **saving time**. While sex and money still plays a part, their interest is much greater than just that.

These types of students want to learn how to fly so they can save time and in their case, save money. When a person is worth thousands of dollars or more an hour, it makes sense to skip the lines at the commercial airport and fly themselves to the next meeting.

This is a very small percentage of what we normally see and very few people ever get this point of accumulated wealth. In addition, many people at this net worth may simply hire a personal pilot to fly them around.

However, they don't need to be a multi-millionaire to fit in this group and it doesn't pertain to just jets. For example, if they were to fly from Philadelphia to Boston using your own plane - say a Cirrus, a multi-engine, or even a Piper Cherokee - compared to commercial airlines, they could very well save time in that you'll be skipping checking in, going through TSA, and waiting at the gate for the next flight.

They'd just simply hop in their own plane and fly to their destination, shaving a few minutes to a few hours out of their commute.

While not overly common, this is still another reason to consider when you're defining your ideal customer, the messaging you're going to use, and where you're going to be marketing your business on different media and platforms online.

So let's put these concepts in the top of our mind as we think about the 3Ms. When we're defining our target customer, what is more important for them? Career or social status? Saving time or saving money?

Understanding their "why?" will help you refine your message so that way it can resonate with your target audience.

The Sales Process

The next thing we'll go over is the sales process and how marketing has its place in the sales process. Growing your business and welcoming new student pilots to your flight school involves a sales process. We need to approach growing our school with the mindset that this is a sales process and that there are specific touchpoints we need to have with each customer. We need to have defined stages in our company for the customer journey from **inbound lead stage** all the way through to **active student pilot stage** where the student is flying multiple times a week with an instructor.

While every business is different and may have different ways of categorizing the steps in their sales process, I find that it most likely evolves and takes similarity to the following stages:

1. Curiosity
2. Enlightenment
3. Commitment

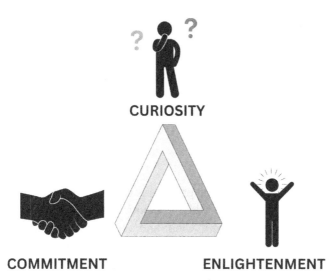

*Figure 2-2. The sales process.
Curiosity, Enlightenment, and then Commitment.*

Curiosity

At the beginning of the sales process, prospective students are often fueled by **curiosity**. This is the moment when your marketing efforts act as a beacon, capturing attention and sparking interest. Whether through compelling social media content, engaging blog posts, or targeted advertising, your goal is to ignite the spark of curiosity that prompts individuals to explore what your flight school has to offer. Effective marketing at this stage sets the foundation for the entire sales journey.

Enlightenment

Moving beyond curiosity, the next phase is one of enlightenment. As potential students seek more information, they enter a stage of deeper exploration and understanding. Marketing steps into the role of an informative guide, providing clear and accessible information through various channels. Your website, brochures, and marketing materials become crucial tools, presenting the advantages of choosing your flight school and addressing the specific needs and preferences identified in your ideal customer personas. This stage is about nurturing interest and facilitating a deeper understanding of the value your flight school provides.

Commitment

The final stage of the sales process is commitment. Here, marketing serves as the bridge that moves potential students from interest to enrollment. Clear and persuasive calls to action, personalized communications, and targeted promotions play a pivotal role in encouraging commitment. Whether it's a special enrollment offer, a trial flight opportunity, or a personalized message highlighting the unique aspects of your flight school, effective marketing ensures that the transition from enlightenment to commitment is smooth and compelling. At this stage, the narrative crafted earlier — your Unique Value Proposition — takes focus and emphasizes why your flight school is the ideal choice.

Understanding and optimizing this journey from curiosity to commitment allows you to tailor your marketing strategies at each stage. By aligning your messaging with the evolving needs and interests of potential students, you create a seamless and persuasive pathway that maximizes the impact of your marketing efforts and enhances the overall success of your flight school.

What Makes Flight Schools Different?

Flight schools have a unique challenge in that **the sales process is much longer** and the curiosity, enlightenment, and commitment phases are actually repeated at minimum twice before you can claim a prospective customer to be a student at your flight school.

The First Commitment

The first commitment step is doing an introductory flight, it's the first transaction, of hopefully many, where your customer pays you for your service. This is your chance to showcase to your future student the opportunity that lies before them: becoming a certificated pilot.

The general feeling out there is that aviation is out of reach for most people. While there is a higher barrier to entry than most activities, people still spend equal amounts of their money on other hobbies like hunting, boating, and cars. Your job is to make it worth it for them to learn to fly.

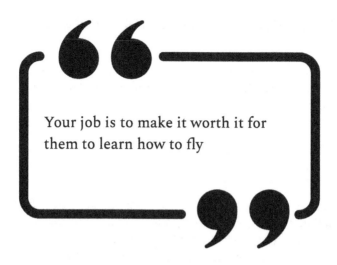

> Your job is to make it worth it for them to learn how to fly

The Second Commitment

After the introductory discovery flight and a post flight briefing, this is your biggest chance to convert this interested prospect into a student that trains at your flight school repetitively. The question worth asking is do you have a documented process of what happens after the discovery flight?

Steps After the Introductory Discovery Flight

First, we need to remove the idea that your CFIs are just CFIs. In the entire discovery flight process they are not only acting as pilot in command giving instruction to a new student, they are also taking on the role as a salesman representing your company.

In addition, your administrative staff and support team members also need to put on the salesman hat as well. This is because any team member that has any contact with your prospective customers is going to directly influence their decision on whether or not they are going to train at your school.

Throughout the discovery flight process, you've shown them the excitement of flight, some general information on how to become a pilot, and what to expect if they decide to start training at your flight school.

Towards the end of their visit, someone needs to ask the $15,000 question: do you want to get paired up with an instructor and get your pilot certificate?

This question, also known as "the close" in salesman land has three possible answers:

1. Yes! I want to start pilot training now
2. No, I didn't enjoy it. It's not right for me.
3. I'm not sure yet.

While we all wish for their answer to be the first one, many times you'll get answers two and three. Let's address each one.

I Want to Start Pilot Training Now

Great. This is what you want to hear. Take them through your onboarding process and get them doing ground school or up in the air as frequently as possible. Whether that's getting documents, signing renter's agreements, getting renter's insurance, completing TSA verification, or creating a profile in your scheduling software; make the process as easy as possible. Revisiting salesman land again here - this is known as reducing the friction of payments. Having online forms, checklists, pamphlets, etc. are all methods you can use to reduce the friction. Optimize your process and make the onboarding process as enjoyable as possible. I even have a flight school that gives away branded backpacks with their logo containing all the marketing materials and school information inside to their new students. This backpack of course is then used to put their newly purchased ground school kit in.

No, I Didn't Enjoy It. It's Not Right for Me.

This is a totally acceptable answer. Being a pilot is not right for everyone. Some people hate the feeling of being suspended in the air in a noisy vibrating machine. However, if you're finding that a large portion of your intro flights are saying this, then you're going to want to look at your process. It might not be just the flying, but also the impression you may have given them which made them feel discouraged. **Here's a simple checklist of addressable items to improve the discovery flight process.**

- Were they able to find your address easily? Are you in a convenient location? If your school is an hour's drive away, it may dissuade them from wanting to commute that far. Or if your flight school is nestled deep within the airfield with no signage helping them as to where to go, they may have felt fear and anxiety traversing around your airport.
- Were your office areas, study areas, bathrooms, and hangars clean and tidy? If your workspace is cluttered and disorganized, you're going to appear disorganized. How are they supposed to trust you with their lives in the air if you can't keep your hangar clean?
- Did your staff (CFIs, maintenance, front desk, etc.) appear happy and enthusiastic? If you have disgruntled employees, you need to have hard conversations and nip it in the bud. Make sure you vet and qualify each one of your team members

during the hiring process and continue to meet with your team members to assess their morale and their performance. One bad apple will spoil the bunch and ruin your company.

- ✈ Did you fly on a gusty or overcast day? Not everyday is sunshine and rainbows but there are things you can do to reduce the probability of bad weather. Some flight schools only do discovery flights in the morning so there are less thermals and bumps and the wind is much calmer. If you're just wedging intro flights into your flight schedule wherever there may be gaps, you may be seeing that the discovery flights are being done during inopportune times.

While there is no one size fits all answer, take a moment to review your discovery flight process and ensure that you are doing everything in your control to make the visit as memorable and enjoyable as possible.

I'm Not Sure Yet

This is where you need to be able to handle objections. They haven't made a decision yet because the value of flight training is perceived to be not worth it for them. They want to become a pilot, but they're either not ready or they're going to be shopping around and comparing flight schools. If it's the latter, you can refer to the earlier points about improving the discovery flight process.

If it's the former and they're not ready yet, there are usually three things that come to mind.

1. Safety concerns
2. Time commitment
3. Financial burden

Let's start off with the safety concerns. If they are concerned about safety, then you didn't do a good job during the discovery flight. You or your CFI didn't make the passenger feel safe unfortunately.

But maybe you did everything by the book. You followed the checklists, you described emergency procedures, you also did your briefings, and explained things clearly. But they still felt unsafe. Then perhaps flight training is truly not right for them. Move on and try again with the next discovery flight!

However if they felt that you were being safe, and that their fear is internal to them - as in they don't think they could do it and they're not of the caliber required - then it's a good opportunity to address their fears and show them that with your guidance and support, they are able to become a safe proficient pilot.

Next up is the time commitment. They *want* to become a pilot, but they're apprehensive about the effort it takes to become a pilot. They know it's a challenge and they're not sure if they're up for it. In that case, the best policy is honesty. They need to be able to fly a few times a week to really solidify the concepts they learn in the air and retain that knowledge. If they are not able to commit to that, then pilot training may indeed not be right for them.

Be honest about the pilot training process. Let them know that most students do not finish their private pilot training with the minimum 40 hours. You've given them the experience of flying and being on the controls. If it's right for them, they're going to turn around and commit eventually. Make sure you continually follow up with them. Call them directly after a week, add them to your newsletter, and add them into your CRM. No sale is over until they say no.

I Can't Afford Flight Training!

This is a very common reaction. First, it goes back to the "market" we mentioned earlier in the 3Ms. Is this person really your ideal customer?

If they don't have the income to support this or the financial backing through family or loans, then they need to make a commitment to themselves (if they really want this) to make it work anyways.

Offer financing options and all that of course. But also don't be afraid of also suggesting that they save some money first before starting. I can't tell you the number of times I've seen students get halfway through their private pilot training and then end up quitting because they ran out of funds. It would have been better to postpone the flight training, save the money, and then go full throttle with flight training when they're able to. It beats having to relearn and redo all the same lessons because they took a long break while they gathered more resources to pay for flight training.

For me personally, I started taking lessons right after my discovery flight and that's when I realized that this was running my wallet dry. I had a decent job at the time that paid well, but flight training became a major expense. I was committed to finishing, but I knew I had to take a hiatus, save some money, and then resume.

While I stopped flying for about 6 months after that, I still took the time while I was saving up to knock out my private pilot written exam. You too can encourage your prospects to join your group ground school first before even paying for another flight lesson. Have them finish their written first so that when they start flight training, the lessons are more efficient.

Handling Objections

Keep in mind the common objections you might face when trying to close the sale. Write down the best answers to their objections and share it with your CFIs and team. Over time you'll see patterns emerge and then you can start developing better scripts, procedures, and methods to raise your close ratio and get more students on your flight line.

Key Takeaways From Chapter 2

- The three M's are market, message, and medium. Prioritize your market and message first before thinking about marketing tactics and strategy.
- UVP stands for unique value proposition. Does your business have a UVP that separates you from the competition?
- The main motivators of pursuing flight training is sex appeal and financial incentive through a pilot career. There is also a sliver of the population that chooses to pursue flight training to save time.
- All sales processes consist of three steps: curiosity, enlightenment, and commitment. For flight schools, the complete sales process is two cycles of this. The first being a commitment to visit your flight school and doing an introductory flight. The second being a commitment to enroll at your flight school and begin pilot training.
- Ensure your team is trained on sales. Right after the discovery flight is the biggest opportunity to close the sale. Ask them if they want to start pilot training and get them on the schedule!
- Understand the common objections. Be prepared to handle each one. Not everyone is destined to be a pilot and it's for the best if it's not right for them. However, we should make sure we put our best foot forward. Be honest about the process and be patient. Keep following up and remember that no sale is over until they say no.

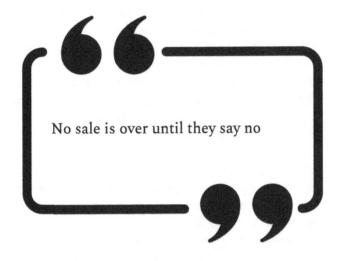

> No sale is over until they say no

Prospective Student Pilot Leads from Your Website

Chapter 3

Your website is the final destination that people interested in flight training will visit. They may have found you on social media from a cool video you posted, or maybe you exhibited your flight school at a career fair or local event and they met you and your team and picked up a brochure. Regardless of how they came into your world, they're eventually going to land on your website.

This chapter is all about how to get them from your website and into your CRM (customer relationship management) software. A CRM, for anyone that is not using one, is your sales infrastructure to track, quantify, and share information about the individuals that have reached out to you with some level of interest in flight training. We'll get more into that in Chapter 9.

Know Your Customer

There's a certain type of person that has an interest in aviation. For many it's fascinating, but there's always going to be a certain demographic that has the courage to take it a step further and do their due diligence about learning how to take their dreams and make it a reality.

Your job is to be there when they start looking and give them the answers they are looking for. Your website should be the gateway of pilot knowledge where newcomers can learn all about the pilot training process.

The website needs to contain certain elements to really get that visitor past window shopping to an actual person at the front desk ready to schedule their next lesson. Let's go over these elements briefly.

The Header

This is the first thing people see when they step onto your website. It usually includes a navigation bar, your phone number, an image or video, and a headline. This headline is also known as the "one liner" which is just a few words that summarizes your business. Donald Miller refers to this in his book *Marketing Made Simple*.

Many flight schools get this wrong and use a headline like, "Follow Your Dreams" or "Elevate Your Career". These types of one liners are vague and don't really specify what your business is about and how it can help your prospect. What you want to do is avoid being artsy or creative with your one liner. Something simple like "Pilot Training in San Diego" is much better because one, it defines your business and how it can help the visitor, and two, it even adds a location keyword into the mix which can help with SEO (search engine optimization). We'll get more into SEO and keywords in Chapter 4.

I also mentioned earlier using a photo or video on the top of the page as well. There's a few things to keep in mind with the media you choose to display on the front page headlines of your website.

1. **Avoid stock imagery** - You want to come across as genuine and real as possible. Use actual photos from your flight school.
2. **Smiling faces leads to better conversions** - A 2014 study published in the psychology research journal *Cognition and Emotion* by Department of Occupational Therapy and Department of Veteran Affairs showed that genuine smiles led to feelings of authenticity, real, attractiveness, and trustworthiness[11].
3. **Be wary of video headers** - While adding a video of a plane taking off or some b-roll footage around your flight school may grab attention, it can lower page speed significantly which hurts SEO and it can also be distracting and make text overlays hard to read. It also may not translate well when viewing a website on a mobile phone. While I'm not completely against video headers, it seems to be overused in our industry. Best web development practices frown upon using video headers and instead suggest using embedded videos farther down the website after the header.

Below are some examples of flight school clients we have where we took these concepts and implemented them. Whether the person is viewing from a mobile device or a computer, the same elements are there: Phone number on top, genuine imagery with smiling team members or students, and a one liner headline with a few words.

Your Pilot Training Academy

Flight school between Alabama and Georgia
Nestled in the heart of Lanett, Alabama
Lanett Municipal Airport 7A3

Figure 3-1. Desktop view of a website header

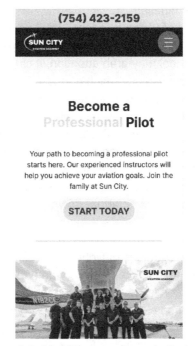

Figure 3-2. Mobile view of a website header

The Stakes and Value Proposition

The next element you're going to add to your website is called the stakes and value proposition. This centers around clearly communicating to potential customers why flight training is not just a skill but a gateway to exciting opportunities and personal growth. Boeing's projections indicate a need for approximately 649,000 new pilots globally by 2042, driven by the exponential growth in air travel and the retirement of current pilots[12].

This demand translates into numerous career paths, from piloting commercial jets to flying for private charters or other pilot career opportunities. For flight schools, effectively articulating this value proposition is important. Highlighting the stakes (such as the increasing global demand for pilots or the diverse career opportunities available) helps potential students see the practical benefits of investing in their aviation education. The decision to enroll in flight training becomes not just a choice but a strategic investment in a rewarding and dynamic career.

Flight schools play a pivotal role in shaping the future pilot workforce. Emphasize your unique strengths: experienced instructors, state of the art facilities, and comprehensive training programs. Flight schools can attract motivated individuals looking to turn their interest in aviation into a profession. This connection between showing why flight training matters and what it offers ensures that flight schools not only train enough pilots for the growing demand but also help new pilots achieve success in their careers.

Your Authority

Establishing your authority in the aviation training industry on your website is crucial to gaining the trust of potential students. Here are some key elements that can help showcase your school's credibility:

- **Expert Instructors**: Highlight the credentials and experience of your instructors. Emphasize their years of flying and teaching expertise, showcasing their ability to provide the best instruction.
- **Accreditations and Certifications**: Display your school's accreditations and certifications prominently. This includes endorsements from organizations like the Aircraft Owners and Pilots Association (AOPA) for excellence in flight training, National Association of Flight Instructors (NAFI) Master CFI designation, and FAA Part 141 certification for structured training programs.
- **Partnerships**: Showcase partnerships with airlines for pilot pathway programs and collaborations with universities like Purdue Global or Liberty University for academic credit transfer. These partnerships validate your school's industry connections and enhance students' career prospects.
- **Industry Recognition**: Highlight any industry awards or recognitions for outstanding training programs, safety records, or contributions to aviation education. These accolades reinforce your school's commitment to excellence and innovation in aviation training.

Additionally, regularly updating your website with informative content such as industry insights, safety tips, and career advice further establishes your authority as a thought leader in aviation education. Showcasing your authority not only attracts potential students seeking reliable information but also solidifies your reputation as a trusted institution dedicated to preparing students for successful careers in aviation.

> Establishing your authority in the aviation training industry on your website is crucial to gaining the trust of potential students.

The Plan

"The Plan" section of your flight school website serves as a roadmap for potential students, outlining the clear steps they'll take on their journey to becoming a pilot. Begin by introducing the pilot training pathway that your school offers, from private pilot certification to advanced ratings like instrument or multi-engine training. Each program should be briefly described to give visitors a clear understanding of your specific flight training process.

In addition, outline the structured path to enrollment and certification. Start with the initial inquiry process encouraging visitors to fill out a website form or contacting you directly. Most flight schools offer an introductory flight lesson or discovery flight to bring new students in.

This section informs potential students how your flight school will guide them through every step of their pilot training journey.

Things That Aren't As Important As You Think

Your website is a sales tool and not a reference manual. I see a lot of flight school websites treat their website as a place to upload very technical and detailed information regarding their aircraft, cite specific regulations, and airport facility directory information. While this may be beneficial for current students and instructors, it's not really doing anything for people that are new to aviation. The potential students are not going to know what useful load is or what a Garmin 430 is. Nor are they going to know what the FAR/AIM is and how that relates to pilot training requirements. I'm not saying to not include it on your website, but keep in mind that some of our pilot jargon isn't going to make sense to newcomers.

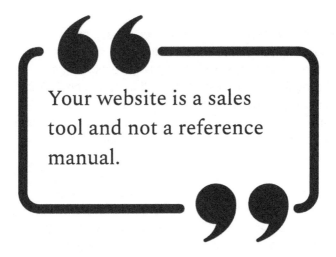

Your website is a sales tool and not a reference manual.

We need to think about how we word certain things and put ourselves in the shoes of someone who has zero knowledge and experience in the aviation industry.

Optimize content for your target audience

Let's consider how to craft your website to convert website visitors into student pilots by structuring your content in such a way that it can persuade visitors to follow your call to actions and give you their contact information. This is also known as **copywriting**. Copywriting is the strategic art of using words to influence, persuade, and ultimately guide readers or users toward a specific action. Whether it's a click, a form submission, a purchase, or any other desired outcome, effective copywriting is the driving force behind these actions[13].

Your offer

When thinking about your website copy, you want to keep in mind that your website is a sales tool. And as a sales tool, the copy needs to center around *your offer*. Your offer encompasses the unique value proposition that sets your flight school apart from competitors and entices potential students to choose your programs.

Effective website copy should communicate this offer in a compelling and concise manner. Clearly articulate the benefits of choosing your flight school, addressing key concerns and aspirations of your target audience. Your offer has to meet the needs and desires of aspiring pilots and set proper expectations for their pilot training in your flight school.

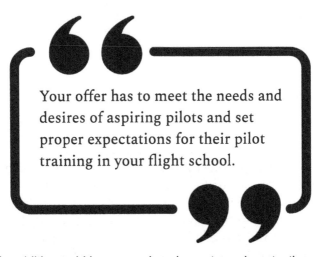

> Your offer has to meet the needs and desires of aspiring pilots and set proper expectations for their pilot training in your flight school.

In addition, add in persuasive elements such as testimonials from successful students and their story of reaching their aviation goals. Include quantitative data that demonstrates your school's track record of success. These elements provide social proof and credibility, reinforcing the value of *your offer* and building trust with website visitors. By strategically aligning your website copy with *your offer*, you can effectively drive conversions on your website and position your flight school as the preferred choice in the competitive aviation training market.

Copywriting Tips

Let's get into our copywriting tips that will take your flight school website to the next level and persuade visitors to choose your school for their aviation training needs. We covered many of them previously in depth so you should start to see emerging patterns when it comes to crafting your website copy for conversions.

- **Highlight the benefits.** Clearly outline the benefits of your flight training programs such as future career opportunities and your industry connections.
- **Use clear and compelling headlines.** Grab attention with concise, benefit driven headlines that convey the value of your programs.
- **Tell stories.** Share success stories and testimonials from past students to build trust and credibility.
- **Use visuals strategically.** Incorporate high quality images and videos of your facilities to enhance engagement and provide a glimpse into the student experience.
- **Showcase expertise.** Highlight the qualifications and experience of your instructors, as well as any industry certifications or affiliations.
- **Create clear calls to action (CTAs).** Guide visitors towards specific actions like scheduling a tour, booking an introductory discovery flight, contacting admissions, or enrolling in your training program.

Create effective call to actions

A call to action (CTA) is a prompt or directive designed to encourage an immediate response or specific action from the person interacting with it. A CTA invites the visitor to take the next step that moves them closer to becoming a student pilot at your flight school. Common examples of CTAs include phrases like "Sign Up Now," "Download Your Free Guide," "Contact Us Today," or "Schedule an Intro Flight." CTAs are essential in guiding potential customers through the sales funnel and prompting them to engage further with your business.

Lead magnets

Remember in Chapter 2 we went over the sales process and how there are three main steps in any sales transaction: curiosity, enlightenment, and commitment. Our CTAs are the pathway to the first commitment step in our sales process.

Enrolling in a $15,000+ pilot training program is a huge ask for most people. We have to bring them into our fold and nurture them to get them over the fence. We begin this process by providing **lead magnets** on our website. Lead magnets are more manageable bite sized resources offered to website visitors in exchange for their contact information. These resources are designed to provide immediate value and address the interests or pain points of our target audience. Some examples of lead magnets include:

- **Free Pilot's Guide**: Offer a downloadable guide that covers essential information for aspiring pilots, such as steps to becoming a pilot, types of pilot licenses, and career opportunities in aviation.
- **Webinar on Aviation Careers**: Host a live or recorded webinar discussing various career paths in aviation, featuring industry experts and success stories from your flight school alumni.
- **Ground School**: Host an in-person group ground school or have pre-recorded video sessions and create an online ground school training program visitors can opt into.
- **Interactive Quiz on Flight Training**: Develop an interactive quiz that assesses visitors' readiness for flight training and provides personalized tips based on their answers.
- **Tour of Flight School Facilities**: Offer a tour that showcases your flight school's facilities, aircraft fleet,

and training equipment, allowing potential students to learn more about your flight school.
- **Discount or Coupon for Introductory Flight Lesson**: Provide a special discount or coupon for visitors to book their first introductory flight lesson with your flight school. Bonus tip: make it a limited time offer.
- **Newsletter Subscription for Flight School Updates**: Invite visitors to subscribe to your newsletter for regular updates on industry news, upcoming events, and exclusive offers from your flight school.

These are all some examples that we've implemented at Right Rudder Marketing for our flight schools that have seen success with lead generation. These forms should stream data into your CRM where you'll put these interested prospects on a nurture campaign and include them in your regularly scheduled email blasts. We'll get into email marketing more in Chapter 7.

Make it easy for them to contact you

In addition to these forms and lead magnets, we want to provide our visitors with multiple methods to get in contact with you. This includes adding your phone number to the top of the website and placing a chat widget on the bottom corner for visitors to fill out.

You can also incorporate pop-up modals that appear on the website after 30 seconds on the page or when the user scrolls up. We went over what to include in your website in terms of content, call to actions, and lead magnets; but another aspect in creating your website is the visual look and feel of the entire website. How things are presented can make or break how a visitor feels about your flight school business and whether or not they'll choose to do business with you.

Design patterns

Let's first talk about how people are browsing your website. We found that with our flight school websites that around 60% of website visitors are browsing the website using their mobile phone. In some websites, this statistic was in the mid 70% where users browsed the website on their mobile device.

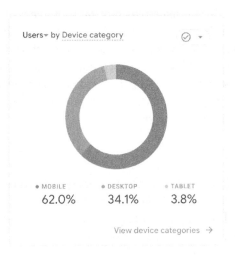

Figure 3-3. Google Analytics of a Right Rudder Marketing flight school website where over 60% of the visitors were browsing the website on their mobile phone.

This is particularly important when considering the design and layout of your website. Does the website fit properly on mobile phones? Google announced in 2018 that they would start ranking sites based on websites that follow the best practices for mobile first indexing[14]. This means that if your website is not mobile friendly, you have less chance of reaching the top three in the Google search results.

> If your website is not mobile friendly, you have less chance of reaching the top three in the Google search results

Mobile Friendly Websites

Google's best practices for mobile first indexing are aimed at ensuring websites are optimized for mobile devices, as Google predominantly uses the mobile version of the content for indexing and ranking. A mobile friendly website should aim to deliver a seamless and enjoyable browsing experience for users accessing the site on their mobile devices, ultimately contributing to higher user engagement, lower bounce rates, and improved conversion rates. Below are some tips to keep in mind when creating your website to ensure that it is mobile friendly and able to get ranked high on search.

- **Responsive Design**: The website layout adapts and adjusts seamlessly to different screen sizes and resolutions, ensuring content remains readable and accessible without the need for horizontal scrolling or zooming.
- **Fast Loading Times**: Mobile friendly websites are optimized for faster loading speeds on mobile networks, reducing bounce rates and improving user engagement.
- **Easy Navigation**: Navigation menus and links are designed to be easy to tap and navigate with a finger on touchscreens, enhancing usability on mobile devices.
- **Readable Text and Images**: Text is legible without zooming, and images are appropriately sized and compressed for quick loading without compromising quality.
- **Optimized Forms**: Forms are designed with mobile users in mind, featuring simplified input fields, auto-fill options, and clear instructions to facilitate easy completion on smaller screens.
- **Cross Browser Compatibility**: Ensuring the website functions consistently across various mobile browsers, including Chrome, Safari, Firefox, and others commonly used on mobile devices.

Images and Media

A key component of designing a website is leveraging your flight school's culture and personality via your media assets. This includes images and videos that capture the spirit of your flight school business. Adding high quality photographs of students smiling or receiving pilot instruction helps with your authority and gives the visitor a sense that your flight school is a real genuine flight school different from the rest.

Using professionally edited video takes this a step further and shows that you're a professional flight school that can be trusted. Don't skimp out on this. Again, avoid using stock imagery.

> Use high quality photos and professionally edited video. Avoid using stock imagery.

UI/UX

UI/UX refers to user interface and user experience. It's a concept that encompasses the design of the website and how users interact with it. It can refer to how buttons are placed, the fonts used, the whitespace in between sections, and how different components are laid out.

The book *Refactoring UI* was published by the creators of Tailwind CSS, a modern CSS framework that many web developers use in newer websites. CSS, or cascading style sheets, is code used in websites that determines the styling and formatting of website elements. In *Refactoring UI*, they describe the different considerations web designers should have when thinking about UI/UX. It provides the design considerations that the newest best looking websites are implementing today.

Some key takeaways from *Refactoring UI* that you should implement in your website design include:

- **Simplicity and Clarity**: Emphasizing the importance of simplicity in design to reduce clutter and enhance clarity. This involves focusing on essential elements and removing unnecessary distractions that can confuse users.
- **Consistency**: Maintaining uniformity in design elements such as colors, fonts, spacing, and interactions across the interface. Consistency helps create a cohesive and intuitive user experience, reducing cognitive load and improving usability.
- **Hierarchy and Visual Weight**: Establishing a clear visual hierarchy to guide users' attention through the interface. This includes using typography, size, color, contrast, and placement to differentiate between primary, secondary, and tertiary elements.
- **Balance and Symmetry**: Achieving visual balance through symmetrical or asymmetrical arrangements of elements. This principle ensures that no single part of the interface feels heavier or out of place, contributing to overall harmony in design.
- **Alignment**: Ensuring that elements are aligned properly to create a neat and organized layout. Aligning elements along a common axis (e.g., left, center, right alignment) improves readability and visual flow.
- **Whitespace (Negative Space)**: Leveraging whitespace around elements to provide breathing

room and improve readability. Whitespace helps prevent overcrowding, enhances content focus, and gives the interface a clean and modern look.
- **Accessibility**: Designing with accessibility in mind to ensure that all users, including those with disabilities, can easily navigate and interact with the interface. This involves using adequate color contrast, providing text alternatives for images, and ensuring keyboard navigability.
- **User Centric Design**: Prioritizing the needs and expectations of users throughout the design process. Understanding user behaviors, preferences, and pain points helps in creating interfaces that are intuitive, efficient, and enjoyable to use.

While there is much more that goes into website design, copywriting, and UI/UX; this chapter encompasses the fundamentals. If you can create a modern professional looking website that has the four main components dialed in (the header, the stakes and value proposition, your authority, and the plan) and have effective call to actions and lead magnets built in; you'll be well on your way to seeing better results and conversions on your website.

Key Takeaways From Chapter 3

- The four main sections to focus on in your website are the header, the stakes and value proposition, your authority, and the plan.
- Your website is a sales tool and the website copy you create should be focused on your offer.
- Leverage strong CTAs (call to actions) and lead magnets to gather contact information from your website visitors.
- Include multiple methods on your website for the visitor to contact you. This includes adding a chat widget and placing your phone number on the top of the page.
- Ensure that your website is mobile friendly and loads fast.
- Use real high quality photographs and professionally edited photos.
- Use UI/UX principles to make your website design easy to digest and interact with.

> Your job is to be there when they start looking and give them the answers they are looking for. Your website should be the gateway of pilot knowledge where newcomers can learn all about the pilot training process.

Search Engine Optimization Hacks

Chapter 4

SEO or search engine optimization is the science of programming websites and resources online to rank businesses on the top of search engines, particularly Google. It's one of my favorite topics so I am excited to dive with you into the world of SEO.

SEO has two main methodologies each contributing to how well your website ranks on search engines. The first is known as on-page SEO. It can also be referred to as technical SEO and it looks at the structure and code of your website. You have direct control of how well you optimize your website because you own the website digital property. You're able to change everything on the website to fit your needs and the search engines' needs.

The second SEO methodology is... can you guess it? Yep, that's right, off-page SEO. While you still have control over this, your control is indirect. This is because off-page SEO refers to everything you do outside of your website. For example, you can add a new description to your Google Business Profile that contains the best keywords related to your target audience, but that doesn't necessarily mean that it will be published. Google administrators have to manually approve each update. Similarly, you can post all you want on your Facebook profile, but in the end it is your audience, Facebook's users, and Facebook's algorithm that determines if a post goes viral or not.

Figure 4-1. The two different types of SEO: on-page SEO and off-page SEO

SEO is always evolving. Especially with the advent of artificial intelligence, search engines and the minds at Google are always updating their ranking algorithm so keep in mind that while the hacks I'll be sharing with you here today may apply at the time that this book was written, you always want to bear in mind different trends and updates that occur in the SEO sphere.

For example, in the previous chapter I had mentioned that in 2018 Google completely switched their ranking mechanism to index websites based on their appearance in mobile phones. SEO techniques had to be adjusted so now we must ensure that our websites are mobile friendly in order to be a major contender in the search engine rankings.

This was not the only update to Google's algorithm. Every year multiple algorithm updates are made. To stay current with Google's algorithm updates, you'll need to stay on top of Google's announcements. You can also check out the publication by the Search Engine Journal where they've documented every single algorithm update since 2003. Even in 2024 there have been multiple updates in regards to spam and artificial intelligence.

https://searchenginejournal.com/google-algorithm-history

Before we dive into on-page and off-page SEO, let's first take a look at a concept called keywords.

Keywords

We're going to touch on this first because determining the right keywords is the first step and lays your foundation for SEO. Keywords are the words inputted into the search field by users. Depending on what the user inputs into the search engine, different links to pages will display in response to the input. The keyword "pilot training near me" will produce different results compared to "flight school near me" so we need to consider all relevant keywords. Let's first take a look at the difference between long tail keywords and short tail keywords.

Types of keywords

There are two types of keywords to bear in mind:

1. Long tail keywords
2. Short tail keywords

Long tail keywords are longer specific keywords that have lower competition and search volume compared to short tail keywords which are shorter keywords that are broad and have more search volume. For example: flight school vs. CFI spin endorsement in Lannett, AL. While short tail keywords have more search volume, they are harder to rank for due to competitor websites that have the same keywords. Compared to long tail keywords which have lower search volumes, long tail keywords are easier to rank for and have a better chance of user engagement and thus website conversions.

The Characteristics of Long-tail Keywords:

1. They consist of more words (which means they are more specific).
2. They usually have lower search volume, but also lower keyword difficulty.
3. They tend to have higher engagement and conversion
4. They are responsible for most of the organic traffic (about 70%)[15].

Therefore it is in our best interest to incorporate long tail keywords into our SEO. When developing your website, publishing a press release, or updating your Google Business Profile, you're going to want to incorporate long tail keywords into your content so that when a user inputs a long tail keyword into the search bar, you show up first.

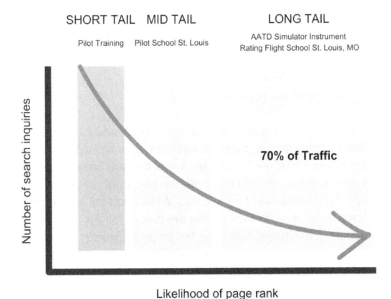

Figure 4-2. Long tail keywords generate 70% of organic website traffic from search engines.

What are your keywords?

Below are the most common keywords that users are searching for when looking for pilot training. We're going to use these keywords as a base to generate longer tail keywords.

- Flight school
- Pilot school
- How to become a pilot
- Pilot academy
- Pilot training process
- Pilot requirements
- Flight lessons
- Aviation school

Next we're going to look at some more specific keywords

- Private pilot certificate
- Instrument rating
- Commercial pilot certificate
- Part 141 flight school
- Affordable pilot training
- Accelerated pilot training
- Introductory flight
- Discovery flight
- Zero to hero pilot training
- AATD simulator

You can see that these keywords are a bit more specific and longer than the previous list. While these keywords have less people searching for them, fewer flight school websites will mention these keywords so it's easier to rank for them. That means that when someone *does* search for them and you have a greater chance of landing in the first page or even top three results which then drives traffic to your website and ultimately leads to higher amount of inquiries and conversions.

Add your location

The last step is mixing in your location to these keywords. For example, if I were a flight school owner in St. Louis and I wanted to rank my instrument rating page on Google, then I would combine the keyword with my location. This equates to "instrument rating St. Louis" or even better, "instrument rating AATD simulator St. Louis." If my instrument rating page has these keywords built in then it has a higher likelihood of getting to the top of Google for users searching for instrument training in St. Louis.

But it doesn't stop there. Don't just stop at using one location keyword. St. Louis and every other city in America has smaller municipalities and localities. In addition to St. Louis, we can add other areas like St. Charles, Belleville,

Maplewood, Ladue, and Clayton. These are names of smaller areas within St. Louis. You're going to want to take a look at all of the different municipalities and localities surrounding your flight school and incorporate them into your keywords.

The keyword lists above are just a brief synopsis of some of the commonly searched keywords for flight training. Right Rudder Marketing has prepared a larger more comprehensive list of keywords available for free on the Right Rudder Marketing website.

Figure 4-3. Right Rudder Marketing's Keyword Guide

To get the free keyword guide, visit our website and download it today. https://rightruddermarketing.com/keywords

Okay so now that we have a good grasp on the keywords we want to optimize for, let's first take a look at on-page technical SEO and then right afterwards, we'll get into off-page SEO tactics.

On-Page SEO

The reason we went over keywords first is because we're going to use these keywords in specific areas of our website. On-page SEO deals with all of the different tweaks and configurations we can do on our website to help search engine robots be able to understand our content better. If the robots are able to understand our content better, we have a higher likelihood of getting ranked for our relevant keywords.

Website Basics

Before we dive into where we're going to inject our keywords, it's worth going through how a website actually works in a technical sense. The topic of web development can encompass tons of books and hours of video tutorials online because it is such a broad topic so we will only touch on this briefly so you have the fundamental knowledge needed to optimize your website for SEO.

When you go on your browser, whether that's on your phone or on your computer, and you type in a web address, what is actually happening is that your browser is making a request to go to a certain server IP address. The server IP address is sometimes referred to as your web hosting provider.

It's like programming your destination airport into your GPS. A website URL or domain name is like the airport identifier and the lats and longs of the airport is the IP address of the website you want to visit.

When your browser receives the actual IP address from the domain servers, it then "directs to" that server and gets a response. This response is usually in the form of an HTML page.

Your browser then receives this HTML page and then renders the content on to your screen. HTML (hypertext markup language) is the code that refers to the elements and content of your website. Besides just text, images, and styling indicators; there is also information that is not visible directly in the browser that is stored at the top and bottom of the HTML file which helps robots, crawlers, and programs to understand the HTML file better.

If we want to turn on every possible switch available to us to help us rank better on the search engines, we're going to have to add the right indications in our meta data and our actual content. These indications and signals (our keywords) are stored in the HTML file via element tags. There are over 100 different types of element tags found in HTML, but we're going to pay greater attention to the ones that help us with SEO.

Side note: You don't need to know how to program or code HTML to benefit from this knowledge. The same tags I am going to reference below can be edited without programming and many page builders and no code options have features where you can type your SEO keyword optimized text into those elements via their interface. Every page builder is different so you might need to do a quick Google search or look into the documentation help files to find where to input your SEO data. Some plugins like Yoast SEO for WordPress help you add this SEO content to your website.

Title

This tag `<title>` is found in the head section of the HTML file. The content you put here will be rendered at the top of the window or tab of the browser. In addition, search engines may use the text you put here when they list your website in their rankings.

For the Right Rudder Marketing Website's homepage our title is programmed as:

```
<title> Right Rudder Marketing | Digital Marketing For Flight Schools </title>
```

As you can see in figure 4-4, the title is rendered at the top of the page. In figure 4-5 you can see that Google took this data and when it listed our page on their search rankings, it copied that same data to list our website.

While you can change this title to your liking, Google's algorithm will at times change how they list your website depending on the content you have on the page. It's not a guarantee that what you put in the `<title>` will be rendered on Google search results, but historically it is what was used and it is still a key factor in determining what text Google will put when they display your website on their search results.

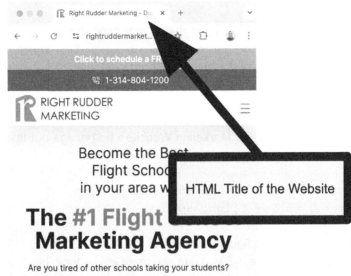

Figure 4-4. Right Rudder Marketing's Homepage HTML Title

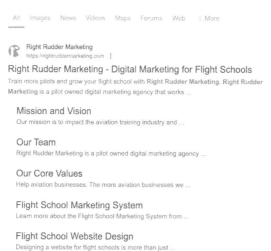

Figure 4-5. Right Rudder Marketing Google Ranking

Your title should describe the webpage and also contain the keywords you want that page to rank for. For example, a flight school in Kansas City should want to put their name and their primary keyword in their title for their home page.

```
<title> Summit Flight Academy | Pilot
Training in Lee's Summit Kansas City </title>
```

In general, you'll want to have your title be around 70 characters long and have the relevant keywords embedded in the text.

This same principle of embedding these keywords into HTML elements apply to the next tag we're going to go over: Headlines

Headlines

Headlines are the text that provides structure to your content. They are programmed as `<h1>`, `<h2>`, `<h3>`, and so on. It provides the outline of your content. These words are typically styled to have a bigger font and a heavier typeface. The `<h1>` tag carries the most weight, then `<h2>` and then `<h3>` and so on. We always want to make sure that they are listed in order of predominance from top to bottom. That is we can structure the headlines like so:

`<h1>Main Header</h1>`
`<p>Content and text</p>`

> **`<h2>Sub Headline</h2>`**
> `<p>Content and text</p>`
>
>> **`<h3> A Smaller Headline</h3>`**
>> `<p>Content and text</p>`
>
> **`<h2>Sub Headline</h2>`**
> `<p>Content and text</p>`

In the above example, we're going from h1→h2→h3→h2. The `<p>` tags are paragraph elements that we would add our content to. We would not go h1→h3→h2→h4. In that case, we skipped from h1 to h3 and missed h2. This confuses search engines and does not follow best practices for accessibility and SEO.

We can always go back up and start again but we cannot skip and step down by more than one. In addition, best practices show that we should only have one `<h1>` per page. Let's say we're working on a page for discovery flights. A good example of how you might structure your page and headlines is below.

`<h1>Your First Flight Lesson In Chicago, IL </h1>`

```
<p>A discovery flight, or introductory flight
is your first flight lesson you will do as a
student pilot.  It's your chance to be at the
controls of the airplane and see if flight
training is right for you.</p>
```

> **`<h2>Flying Over Naperville</h2>`**
> ```
> <p>During the discovery flight, your
> CFI (certified flight instructor)
> will let you take control of the
> Airplane.  You'll see the local area
> and fly over Naperville, Aurora, and
> the surrounding Chicagoland area.</p>
> ```
>
>> **`<h3>How To Schedule Your Discovery Flight</h3>`**
>> ```
>> <p>If you think you're ready to
>> fly, reach out to Chicago Flight
>> School and book today</p>
>> <button>SCHEDULE NOW</button>
>> ```
>
> **`<h2>What to Expect </h2>`**
> ```
> <p>We recommend wearing close-toed
> shoes and bringing a light jacket as it
> may get chilly as you fly overhead
> Chicago and above the Willis Tower.</p>
> ```

As you can see in the above example, we went from h1→h2→h3→h2. In addition, we embedded our keywords into our headlines and content. We used different location keywords besides "Chicago" like "Naperville", "Chicagoland", and "Aurora" and even "Willis Tower." We also used synonyms for "discovery flight" like "your first flight lesson" and "introductory flight" to encompass different possible keywords that might be searched. Keep your keywords in mind when creating your headlines on your web pages.

Embed your keywords in your headlines and content.

Alt Text and Image File Names

We're going to go over images on your website. Alt text is technically not an HTML element tag, but rather a parameter that goes into your images. `alt` is derived from the words "alternate text." When we embed images on a website, the image element tag has this special `alt` attribute that we can program SEO keyword text into. Image element tags are structured as so:

```
<img src={image source} alt="SEO TEXT" />
```

What we should understand is that search engines cannot understand image files as a picture and they rely on the file names and alt attributes to better understand the image and how it relates to the webpage.

While there is emerging AI (artificial intelligence) software that can understand and manipulate images, as of July 2024 there has not been a published Google algorithm update stating that they are using AI to understand images and influence page rankings. Therefore, we need to program our keywords into the file name and `alt` attribute.

Let's take a look at an example.

Figure 4-6. Ideal Aviation Image

In this photo Ideal Aviation, a Right Rudder Marketing flight school partner, has this image on their website. The actual code that is on their website is:

```
<img src="student-pilot-receives-certificate.webp" alt="Student Pilot Passes Private Pilot Checkride at Ideal Aviation">
```

There's a few key takeaways to look at here. First is the file name which is "student-pilot-receives-certificate.webp" where you can see that we've separated the words with hyphens. In addition, we have descriptive keywords embedded in the name like student, pilot, and certificate.

Another thing to look at is that the file extension ends with .webp and not .jpg or .png. .jpg and .png are very common image file types and what you might get when you download images from your camera. However, for websites we want to have the best quality image with the smallest file size to help with page speed. .webp is a file format that is particularly favored by the search engines because it offers superior compression and reduces file sizes to render web pages better.

The next thing to look at is the alt parameter and we can see that "Student Pilot Passes Private Pilot Checkride at Ideal Aviation" has keywords like "student pilot", "private pilot", and "checkride" embedded in the alt parameter.

BONUS TIP: Images also contain metadata like GPS coordinates of where the picture was taken and the device the photo was captured with. Your phone automatically inputs this data into each photo and if you maintain this metadata into your website's version of the image, search engines can also read this data to understand your business better. So if your photo has GPS data embedded in the file, then search engines will start ranking your website for locations around the GPS coordinates.

Meta Description

The next few elements we're going to look at are invisible parts of the website and not rendered anywhere in the browser. The way this works is that these elements are stored in the `<head>` section of a website. A standard HTML file is programmed as below.

```
<html>
    <head>
        {metadata and invisible things}
    </head>
    <body>
        {actual content of the website}
    </body>
</html>
```

The meta description which we'll go over first is put in this `<head>` section of the website. The meta description is a small paragraph that should describe the page. Best practices say that our meta descriptions should be around 160 characters but it is a debated topic among SEO experts with some people saying that having over 300 characters is okay.

Historically, Google and other search engines used this text after the title when listing your site on their search engine results page to give a snippet of the website to the viewer. While this is no longer the case as Google now might choose to use headline text or paragraph text instead to display on their search results, it is still a good opportunity to send a signal to Google and embed keywords.

High Tide Aviation
https://flyhightide.com

High Tide Aviation: Airplane and Helicopter Tours
High Tide Aviation is a full-service aviation company based in **Southport, North Carolina**. We offer **flight training**, aircraft rental, and aircraft ...
Locations · Southport, NC Oak Island · The High Tide Experience · Other Services

hightideaviation.com
https://hightideaviation.com

High Tide Aviation
High Tide Aviation offers **flight schools** and training facilities at both Cape Fear Regional Jetport in **Southport, NC**, and McKinnon St Simons Island Airport on ...

Figure 4-7. High Tide Aviation Search Results

In figure 4-7, we see that below the title text, there is descriptive text about the webpage. In this case, below is the actual code we used for their meta descriptions.

```
<meta name="description" content="High Tide
Aviation is a full-service aviation company
based in Southport, North Carolina. We offer
flight training, aircraft rental, and
aircraft maintenance services." />
```

```
<meta name="description" content="Join the
Southeast Coast's leading airplane and
helicopter training center. High Tide
Aviation in Southport, NC, and St Simons
Island, GA, offers premier flight training
across the southeastern coast.">
```

As you may have noticed, the search results page used the meta description provided for their search results with https://flyhightide.com and on the other hand, for https://hightideaviation.com they pulled actual content from their website instead of listing the meta description.

The thing to keep in mind is that just because the meta description was not copied directly into the search result page does not mean that Google did not read the text and used the data as a signal to rank the websites.

Let's improve your meta descriptions for better page rankings. Make sure that you...

- Don't over emphasize on the number of characters, as Google might pull content instead of the meta description to put on their search ranking pages.
- Do not add duplicate meta descriptions. That is every web page on your website should have unique descriptions.
- Write for your users and encourage them to click with specific and relevant content.
- Add clear CTAs in your meta descriptions like enroll today, book now, contact us today, etc.
- Add your targeted keywords in descriptions.

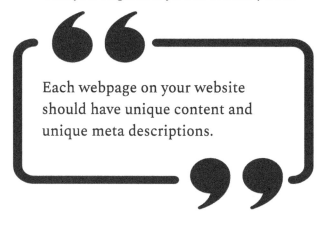

Each webpage on your website should have unique content and unique meta descriptions.

Meta Keywords

Meta keywords are similar to meta descriptions in that they are invisible and found in the `<head>` section of your website. They were originally used by search engines to understand the content of a webpage and help determine its relevance to specific search queries.

In the early days of search engine optimization (SEO), meta keywords were a significant factor in determining page rankings. Webmasters would list relevant keywords in this tag to signal to search engines what the page was about. Over time, the meta keywords tag was widely abused by webmasters who stuffed it with irrelevant or repetitive keywords in an attempt to manipulate search rankings. As a result, major search engines like Google, Bing, and Yahoo have de-emphasized or completely ignored the meta keywords tag in their ranking algorithms.

However, I still think that it's worth adding it in the `<head>` section anyways as it doesn't hurt rankings and may have some benefit. At Right Rudder Marketing, we make sure that each page has unique keywords added to this section. Staying with the High Tide Aviation example we used earlier, this is the format of how to add Meta Keywords.

```
<meta name="keywords" content="Southeast Coast flight training, Southport NC pilot school, St Simons Island GA flight instruction, airplane training Southeast, helicopter lessons Southeast Coast">
```

Schema

Schema is also found in the `<head>` section. It provides detailed information about the website's content and purpose in a JSON format, helping search engines understand and display this information more effectively. Schema is another place to insert keywords and it is a powerful tool to enhance the visibility and appearance of your website in search results.

Schema.org provides an official publication that outlines every attribute commonly accepted and used by search engines. Using the right schema parameters can unlock special features on Google, such as rich snippets and widgets, which can appear on the search result page and enhance your Google Business profile.

Consistent Updates and Blog Posts

You never want to just create a website and let it sit indefinitely on the internet with no updates. While revamping, updating, and adding content to your website frequently is the best way to keep signaling to search engines that you're relevant, it can be time consuming to do so. An easy way to keep pushing more content into your website is to add a blog into your website. Adding blog articles helps lengthen your sitemap and web presence.

You don't need to overthink it. Just push something out at least once a month and you're already going to be doing better than most flight schools.

In the book *They Ask, You Answer* Marcus Sheridan goes over how to think about your content creation strategy and it revolves around the concept of providing content that your target audience is looking for. "Content—assuming it is honest and transparent—is the greatest sales tool in the world today" according Marcus. So provide good content that your customers are looking for. We've done blog posts in the past about VORs, alternate minimums, tips for landing, and explanations of the traffic pattern. Whatever you choose to write about, the key concept is to stay consistent and keep publishing content every month.

Additional On-Page SEO Hacks

The final and last part we'll talk about in regards to on-page SEO is pagespeed. Pagespeed is another big signal to Google and has a high impact on the Google ranking algorithm. Pages that load faster and more likely to get better rankings. This is because Google wants to provide their users with websites that are relevant, answer their questions, and have good user experience. A slow website is a bad user experience. It is commonly accepted that if a website takes more than a couple seconds to load, the user is likely to hop off and look for another website.

A big drawback to using no-code editors like WordPress, Wix, and GoDaddy is that in order to render a website, the entire page building engine has to be loaded every single time the website is visited online. This in turn lowers the page speed. Coding a website from scratch and using modern professional web development tools and technologies yield a better pagespeed score and in turn, have a better chance of ranking higher.

> Coding a website from scratch and using modern professional web development tools and technologies yield a better pagespeed score and in turn, have a better chance of ranking higher

Learning how to code takes years of experience and may not be feasible for flight school owners just looking to get a webpage up. In that case, using WordPress or similar page builders is an acceptable option. But bear in mind that by going this route, you are leaving tons of opportunities for better rankings on the table.

Check out https://pagespeed.web.dev/ which is an online tool published by Google that measures page speed. It also provides additional technical insights in regards to accessibility, best practices, and SEO. If you're running a WordPress site, the highest I've ever seen a score is 58 out of a 100. By coding a website from scratch, we consistently see page speeds above 70 with many of our flight schools hitting in the 90s and 80s. If you run the audit and you see all red, then you know that there is work that needs to be done.

Tracking Progress

You can always manually search a specific keyword like "helicopter school Orlando" and see where your flight school pops up in search results.

But it's worth mentioning that there are online tools that help provide data measuring your rankings on Google search. Most notable software includes products like Semrush, Moz, and Ahrefs. Using these tools, you can track how many keywords you rank for and your position. In addition, you can take a look at how your neighboring flight schools are doing as well. These tools also provide solutions for fixing your on-page SEO and can do audits looking at the titles, headlines, alt text, meta description/keywords, and schema.

Off-Page SEO

All of the above tactics revolved around changing and updating your website to include keywords that make it easier for search engines to understand your website and in turn help with ranking your website higher. The other part of SEO is off-page SEO which we'll get into in the next chapter.

Key Takeaways From Chapter 4

- There are two main methodologies of SEO: on-page and off-page. On-page refers to the technical details you embed on your website and off-page refers to everything you do outside of your website.
- Come up with a list of keywords that you want to rank your website for. Keep in mind different synonyms for words, surrounding localities and municipalities, and also utilizing long tail keywords.
- Long tail keywords have lower search volumes but more traffic so it's less competition, easier to rank for, and increases likelihood of conversions. Make your pages specific and targeted instead of general and broad.
- Your title for your page should include relevant keywords and may be used to list your page on search engine results pages.
- Headlines help robots and page crawlers understand your content. They should have keywords embedded in them. They should also be listed in order of predominance and not skip.
- Images should have keywords embedded in the file name and alt attribute. Images should be compressed into .webp format.
- Add meta description and keywords to the `<head>` section of your website.
- JSON schema on your website provides another place to input keywords for search engine crawlers to understand your website.
- Coding a website from scratch compared to no-code page builders like WordPress leads to higher and faster pagespeed scores.

> Google wants to provide their users with websites that are relevant, answer their questions, and have good user experience.

Ranking Top on Google Maps and Search

Chapter 5

The previous chapter went over all of the things we can do inside our website to rank high on Google search. And that's only half the story. We're going to get into off-page SEO in this chapter which is all about everything you can outside your website to get higher results in search.

Google Business Profile

A Google Business Profile (GBP), also referred as Google My Business (GMB), is a directory listing with Google. This listing allows for you to be listed with Google Maps. Most flight schools have one created already. If not, Google or your customers likely may have started one for you.

Just creating the listing doesn't do much as far as ranking on top, but it gets you in the game at least since it allows you to start ranking on Google Maps. There are a few things we can tweak and optimize so that you have a better chance of ranking on Google Maps.

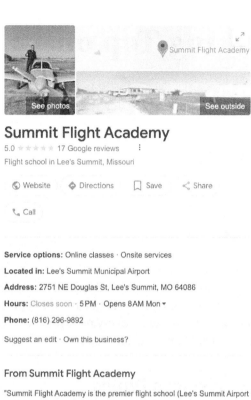

Figure 5-1. Google Business Profile Example

Description

Many flight school owners use this section to talk about their business. They'll mention things like their experience and how many years they've been in business. They'll talk about their accolades and awards. They'll say things like "we have the best modern fleet available!" Unfortunately, this is the wrong way to go about it. While doing the above may provide insightful information about your flight school and your experience, it does not optimize for better map rankings and organic search results.

When thinking about what to put in your GMB description, there are two things we want to look out for:

1. Your services
2. Where you are

This is all going back to keywords again. The best GMB descriptions have specific services offered at and locations of your school. When drafting your GMB description add keywords like:

- Airline pilot training
- Private pilot certificate
- Instrument rating
- Commercial pilot certificate
- Multi-engine rating add on
- Certified flight instructor (CFI)
- Airline transport pilot (ATP)

For your location keywords add the main city, local municipalities, your airport name, and airport identifier.

Last thing to mention is that you have a total of 750 characters you can use when crafting your GMB description. And the first 250 is what is immediately visible in the Google profile with the rest requiring the user to click "more" (see Figure 5-1 for an example of this truncation).

The entire GMB description that we used for Summit Flight Academy in Kansas City, MO is as follows:

Summit Flight Academy is the premier **flight school** (**Lee's Summit Airport KLXT**) offering professional, career track **flight training** in **Kansas City**, reaching from **Overland Park** to **Olathe**. From **private pilot certification** to advanced training including **instrument rating, commercial pilot certificate**, instructor certificates (**CFI, CFII, MEI**), and complete career track **zero to hero pilot training programs**. Enroll at our **Lee's Summit, Missouri**, location for top-notch **flight training programs** and **become a pilot** today!

I highlighted all of the relevant keywords in the GMB description. This description is jam packed with keywords and it helps rank Summit Flight Academy higher on Google search and Google Maps.

Category and Services

The primary category you're going to want to list your business as is "flight school". You can also list it as a secondary category "aviation training institute" in your GBP. Then after selecting your categories, you list all of your services and training programs offered. Be as comprehensive as possible. You don't need to use the Google provided services. You can add customized service keywords if Google doesn't provide an option you're looking for.

Most users will not see this portion of the profile, however, it does help with SEO so make sure you complete this part!

Figure 5-2. Google Business Profile menu options

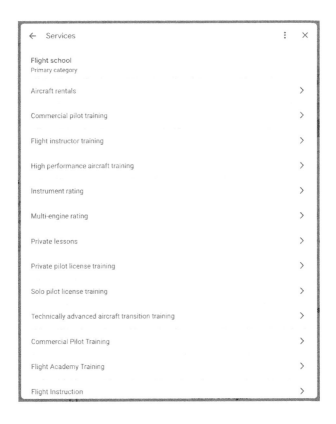

Figure 5-3. Google Business Profile services listed under the "flight school" business category

You can adjust your business category by clicking "Edit Profile" and the services you list will go under "Edit Services."

Products

This one is often neglected. You can double up on the services and add them into products too. Just click "Edit Products" as seen in Figure 5-2 in the bottom left. With products, you can add paragraphs of information specific to your service offering and add a link to your website.

Figure 5-4. Google Business Profile add product interface

GMB Add Product Tips:

- Use keywords in the product name and product description.
- Add a photo for better visual appearance. Keep in mind the filename of the image. Add keywords to the filename too! Bonus points if your image has meta GPS data.
- Add a link to your website in the "Product landing page url" text field.

When you add products it looks like this:

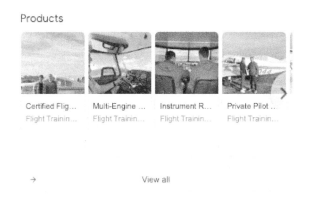

Figure 5-5. GMB products carousel

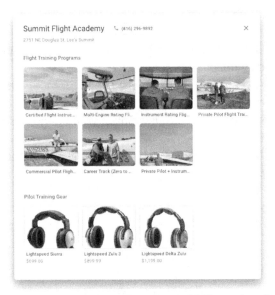

Figure 5-6. Summit Flight Academy GMB product listing

Certified Flight Instructor Training

At Summit Flight Academy, we take immense pride in nurturing the next generation of aviation professionals through our comprehensive Certified Flight Instructor (CFI) training programs. Certified Flight Instructors play a pivotal role in shaping the skills and knowledge of aspiring pilots, serving as mentors, guides, and educators. Our CFI training courses are designed to equip you with the necessary expertise to become an influential and respected instructor, capable of imparting invaluable knowledge and instilling a culture of safety, proficiency, and excellence in your students.

 Visit site

Figure 5-7. GMB product listing for CFI training

Updates and Posts

Every flight school we've worked with and all the flight schools' GMB profiles I've seen never add this feature in. Adding an update is an easy way to keep your GBP fresh and signals to Google that you're in business and relevant. You could add typical things that you'd also post on social media like solos, checkride passes, and events.

A technique that has worked well for our flight schools is copying over the first paragraph or so of a blog post into the GMB update. Adding an update in GMB also allows you to input a URL so we usually link back to the blog post.

Figure 5-8. GMB update example

Name Address Phone Number

As far as SEO goes for basic business details in your GMB profile, we have just a few suggestions.

- Don't use a 1-800 toll free number. (Because 1-800 numbers are used by a lot of scammers and telemarketers reducing your authority.)
- Don't choose 24 hours for your business hours. (Because Google would think you never changed the default business hours.)
- Stay consistent. When you list your business on other directories (we'll get into this later in this chapter), make sure your NAP (name/address/phone) is the same in all your listings.
- Make sure your address is valid and Google Maps matches the location in the map to the actual address.

Reviews

We saved the best for last. Reviews can be considered the digital currency for your GMB profile. Typically the more reviews you have, the higher you will rank. A business with low reviews but higher quantity of reviews will outrank a business with a perfect 5.0 but has only a handful of reviews. Don't be afraid to ask your students to leave a review.

The best times we've found to ask our students to leave a review are:

- After a discovery flight
- After a student solo
- After a checkride pass

This is because typically, students are emotional and very happy which leads to more detailed and enthusiastic 5 star reviews. Make sure you respond to all reviews too.

Responding to Negative Reviews

Inevitably, you're going to receive a negative review once in a blue moon. It's important to respond to all reviews, especially negative ones. When addressing negative reviews, frame your response not just for the reviewer, but for other people who are looking at your Google profile. Potential customers will read your responses to see how you handle criticisms and whether you are professional, empathetic, and committed to resolving issues. Well crafted responses can demonstrate your dedication to customer satisfaction and turn a negative impression into a positive one.

I was talking to Omar Amin, the owner of OC Flight Lessons, one of the top flight schools in Orange County, California. He mentioned to me that he once received a negative review and responded to the review. A few months later, he was talking to some prospective students and they mentioned that they chose his flight school because of the review response he left. This just goes to show that responding to negative reviews pays dividends when done correctly.

In addition, consistently getting five star reviews can significantly lessen the impact of a single negative review. A profile with 100+ reviews will not be as affected by one negative comment as a profile with only 10 reviews. Consistently encourage satisfied customers to leave positive reviews to build a strong overall rating. This not only boosts your reputation but also helps buffer against the occasional negative feedback. A high volume of positive reviews showcases your flight school's commitment to excellence and can reassure potential customers that your negative reviews are exceptions rather than the norm.

Online Directories

Online directories are valuable tools for increasing your flight school's visibility and credibility. These platforms list businesses in specific categories, making it easier for potential students to find your services. By ensuring your flight school is listed in relevant directories, you increase your chances of being discovered by people actively seeking flight training. Popular online directories include Yelp, Yellow Pages, Bing, and Apple Maps.

There are aviation-specific directories as well like AOPA Flight School Finder, Pilot Training USA, FlightSchoolList.com, Aviation Schools Online, Best Aviation, AvScholars, GlobalAir.com, SkyTough, Learn to Fly USA, Pilot Career Centre, Flying Mag's Flight School Directory.

Search engines often regard listings in reputable directories as a sign of legitimacy and trustworthiness. Ensure that your business information (name, address, phone number, and website) is consistent across all directories. This consistency helps search engines verify your business details, which can positively influence your search rankings. Include detailed descriptions, high quality photos, and accurate contact information in your listings.

Finally, online directories often feature review sections where students can leave feedback about their experiences with your flight school. Positive reviews on these platforms can significantly boost your reputation and attract more students. Encourage satisfied students to leave reviews and monitor these platforms regularly to respond to feedback. Engaging with reviews, both positive and negative, demonstrates your commitment to customer satisfaction and helps build trust with potential clients. By leveraging online directories effectively, you can expand your reach, improve your SEO, and enhance your flight school's reputation.

Press Releases

Press releases are a great way to get the word out about your flight school and grab attention. They can help you share big news like new planes, partnerships, student achievements, or events. By sending out press releases, you can get local newspapers, aviation magazines, and even potential students to notice your school. This can make your flight school look like a top choice for training.

When writing a press release, keep it simple and clear. Start with an interesting headline, followed by a short summary, and then the main details. Explain who is involved, what is happening, when and where it will take place, and why it's important. Adding quotes from people at your school, like the owner or an instructor, can make the story more relatable. Including good photos or videos can also help catch people's eyes. Lastly, make sure there are links on the press release that go back to your website! Make sure to send your press release to the right places, like news websites and aviation blogs.

Sending out press releases regularly keeps your flight school in the spotlight and shows that you're active and successful. This is good for building trust with potential students who might be checking out your school. By using press releases, you can boost your school's reputation, get more media coverage, and attract more students. Typically, you can get a press release done for a few hundred bucks. We usually aim to get one press release per quarter for each of our flight schools.

Backlinks

Backlinks are links from other websites that point to your flight school's website. They are important because they can help your site rank higher on search engines like Google. When trusted websites link to your site, it shows search engines that your content is valuable. This makes it easier for people to find your flight school when they search online.

One way to get good backlinks is by partnering with other businesses and organizations. For example, you can partner with local aviation clubs, aircraft manufacturers, or flight training associations. Ask them to link to your website from theirs. You can also write articles for their websites and include a link back to your site. This not only helps with backlinks but also builds strong relationships in the aviation community. We've also reposted some of our content to places like Reddit and LinkedIn.

Don't forget about your home airport. Many airports have websites that list all the businesses based there. Make sure your flight school is listed and ask them to add a link to your website. This is a simple way to get a valuable backlink and attract local students who visit the airport's website.

Working on getting backlinks regularly can really help your flight school. The more quality backlinks you have, the better your site will rank in search results. This means more people will see your flight school when they search for flight training. By focusing on backlinks, you can get more visitors to your website and attract more students.

Backlink Risks

Buying backlinks from services like Fiverr or Legitt can be tempting because it seems like a quick way to boost your website's ranking. However, this approach can be risky and may do more harm than good. Search engines like Google have strict guidelines against buying backlinks. If they detect that your website has purchased links, you could face penalties that can hurt your search rankings or even get your site removed from search results altogether.

We tried this in the past and then looked at our results on Semrush and it showed that by going this route, it added toxicity to our domain authority.

Instead of buying backlinks, focus on building them naturally. Create high quality content that others want to link to, such as informative blog posts, helpful guides, or engaging videos about flight training. Reach out to aviation bloggers, local news sites, and industry publications to share your content and ask for links. Building genuine relationships with other businesses and organizations can also lead to valuable backlinks that are both safe and effective.

In the long run, earning backlinks naturally is a more sustainable and trustworthy strategy. It not only helps improve your search engine rankings but also builds your flight school's reputation. By focusing on providing value and fostering real connections, you can attract more students and grow your flight school without risking penalties from search engines.

Key Takeaways From Chapter 5

- Claim your GBP and add keyword embedded content to all of the GBP options like products and updates.
- The more reviews you have, the higher you will rank.
- Respond to positive reviews and negative reviews. For negative reviews, keep in mind that your reader is not the reviewer but other people that might come across your profile in the future.
- List your business in online directories to increase your web presence.
- Publish press releases whenever you have newsworthy events at your flight school.
- Continually scout for backlinks, links on other websites that go to your website. Be wary of fast and easy solutions on Fiverr and Legitt.

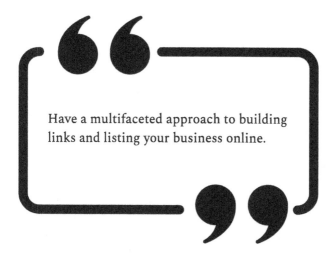

> Have a multifaceted approach to building links and listing your business online.

Social Media Marketing

Chapter 6

Social media is an important tool for marketing your flight school. It helps businesses connect with people, share their message, and attract customers. For flight schools, social media is a powerful way to reach potential students and show what makes your school special. By using social media, you can grow your flight school and build a strong online presence.

We're going to go over how you should think about social media and how to leverage this tool for your business. We're not going to get into advertising just yet. That's in Chapter 9. Instead, we're going to look at how to use social media to build an audience and community organically.

There are many social media platforms out there, like Facebook, Instagram, Twitter, LinkedIn, TikTok, and YouTube. Each platform has its own features and audience that we want to pay special attention to. Remember in Chapter 2 we went over the 3Ms? Your *market* should be targeting your ideal customers. Where does your ideal customer spend their time online?

If you are targeting fresh out of high school students or college aged students, then Instagram and Tik Tok are popular platforms that they spend a lot of time on. On the other hand, if you are targeting high wealth individuals that are in the middle or end of their career, then Twitter, LinkedIn, and Facebook are known to have more senior demographics. Youtube has a pretty wide spread and has viewers from all demographics.

Similar to listing your website and business in online directories like we mentioned in the previous chapter, setting up your social media profiles helps you to get noticed and connect with people who are interested in learning to fly.

The end goal of using social media is simple: Get more leads. Whether they contact you directly on Facebook or they click a link on your profile that directs them to your website, we need to keep our eyes on the target.

Let's discuss how to use social media to create engaging content and build your audience. By the end of this chapter, you will have a clear plan for using social media to attract more students and grow your flight school.

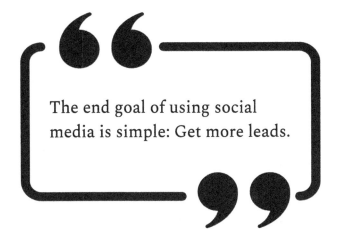

The end goal of using social media is simple: Get more leads.

Create Your Profiles

When setting up your social media presence, it's important to leverage both a personal and a business profile. A business profile represents your flight school and allows you to share official updates, promotions, and professional content. Some platforms provide tools and analytics that can help you understand your audience and measure your social media success. On the other hand, a personal profile is all about you as an individual. This profile is treated as a "regular user" on the social media platform. A personal profile is where you can share your personal stories, experiences, and connect with people on a more personal level.

Using both personal and business profiles is a powerful strategy for promoting your flight school. Your business profile is essential for maintaining a professional image and providing important information about your services. Conversely, your personal profile can add a layer of authenticity and trust. When you share your own experiences and passion for flying, it makes your business more relatable and trustworthy. Prospective students are more likely to connect with you and feel confident in choosing your flight school.

To make the most of this strategy, it's important to post relevant content on each profile. Use your business profile to post official updates, promotions, and professional content related to your flight school. On your personal profile, share your journey, personal insights, and behind the scenes perspectives with your life in aviation. Cross promote your content to drive traffic between your profiles and create a cohesive online presence. By leveraging both profiles effectively, you can build a strong personal brand while also promoting your flight school. Typically, you will have more reach with your personal profile compared to your business profile.

Content is King

The quote "Content is king" is originally from an essay Microsoft founder Bill Gates wrote in 1996. In it, he describes the future of the Internet as a marketplace for content. The phrase "content is king" is not new, but because of the increased focus on content marketing strategies, the quote is commonly used. Gary Vaynerchuck, a well known businessman and internet personality, elaborated further and said that "content is king, but context is God" meaning that when we create content and post it online, we need to be mindful of what platform we're using and the reason why users on said platform are there.

Different platforms have different purposes. What works on Facebook might not work as well on Instagram or YouTube. Tailor your content to fit each platform's strengths. For example, videos on YouTube are great for long form content and explaining things. This can be things like a recording of a group ground school session, interviews with students and staff, or a documentary about your flight school and your programs.

On the other hand, Youtube Shorts, Facebook, Tik Tok, and Instagram are great for short form videos. These platforms are perfect for quick updates, behind the scenes glimpses, student testimonials, or engaging snippets of flight training sessions. Short form videos are effective in capturing attention quickly and driving engagement among viewers who prefer concise, visually compelling content.

In my experience, many viewers enjoy seeing actual flight time footage in particular landings so strap on a go pro and get some footage to be cut up later.

A quick note about short form content. Your goal with creating short form content is to "stop the scroll." This means that the first 3 seconds of your video needs to have a strong hook. Start with a visually striking scene, an intriguing question, or a captivating moment from a flight lesson to draw viewers in and encourage them to watch the entire video. Create a strong hook with your short form content to reel in the viewer and keep them engaged.

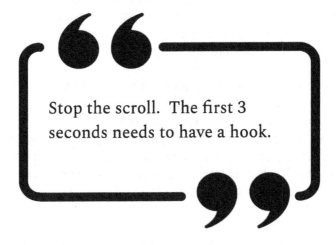

Stop the scroll. The first 3 seconds needs to have a hook.

Authenticity and Genuineness

Social media is you get to show your audience and prospective student pilots who you really are and what your flight school is all about. When you share real stories and experiences and show to the world your passion for aviation and dedication to student success, you build trust and credibility. Posting regular updates about actual flight lessons, including student achievements like solo flights or checkride passes allows prospects to glimpse into how your flight school operates and the culture that you've built with your business.

Consistency

Matt, a flight school owner that had reached out to me for advice regarding marketing for his flight school asked me how often he should post content on social media. I responded and said as frequently as possible. A good way to look at this is treating it like the lottery. Except your chances of winning are much higher! And this is free compared to a lottery ticket.

90% of your social media posts will be a flop and go unnoticed or have little views. However, all it takes is one captivating post to surge and have a bit of virality. Also, don't limit yourself to just aviation related posts. For example, at one of the flight schools I fly at, the owner is an elderly man well into his 70s. However, he is part of a softball team for senior folks and they actually compete with other senior softball teams. I encouraged him to go ahead and create a post showing off a clip or two of him and his team playing softball on his business facebook account. That post received more likes and views compared to their normal content.

When you post things that are outside of aviation, you start to branch out to larger audiences which widens your net and has the potential to bring in a higher volume of leads. For example, there is a person who has never been involved with or followed aviation type content and was instead a big fan of softball. When that person sees your post relating to softball and then checks out your profile which is surrounded by aviation and flight training content, then that person is now exposed to a world he or she would have never searched for.

In addition, if you post frequently you're going to run out of flight training and aviation related content. Feel free to branch out and post about your children, pets, family, friends, and other hobbies that you might enjoy. You never know who will see the video and it might lead to another student at your flight school.

Let's put it in perspective. You or your team might spend 15 to 30 minutes preparing a short video to be uploaded on Instagram. In essence, this video is free or negligible to your P&L. However the payoff is huge. If you get a new prospect into your circle and they convert into a student pilot, then you just made $15,000 out of just simply posting a quick video.

If I was a statistician, then I'd realize that these odds are definitely in my favor and post every day!

The key is being consistent. Don't neglect your social media profiles. If your last post is over a year old, then when people look your flight school up to learn more about your business, they're going to think you went out of business and are no longer offering services.

Your Message

I'm going to bring up the 3Ms again and talk about *messaging*. For flight schools, effective messaging involves clearly communicating what makes your school unique and why prospective students should choose your program (your UVP -> unique value proposition). Your messaging should emphasize your school's strengths, such as experienced instructors, well maintained aircraft, and successful graduates. It should resonate with your audience's aspirations and needs, addressing their concerns and highlighting the benefits of training at your institution.

Figure 6-1. The 3Ms of Marketing: Market, Message, and Medium

You'll want to encapsulate your message into your branding and culture. That is, you'll want to have consistent visual themes. Using the same fonts, colors, and style across all your social media channels ensures that your audience can instantly recognize your content, whether they see it on Facebook, Instagram, or LinkedIn. This visual coherence not only strengthens brand recognition but also conveys a sense of professionalism and attention to detail, which are important qualities in aviation education.

Your Plan For Social Media

A lot of flight school owners over think social media. They want to put out the best content and receive many views, likes, and followers. I'm here to tell you that in the grand scheme of things, it's not really all that important. From an SEO perspective, social media only contributes about 2-5% in regards to signals to google[16] and is not that big of a factor in rankings. Don't get it in your head that you need to have

100K+ followers or thousands of views and likes. Just create the profile, post on it regularly, and be genuine. You'd rather have 500 followers that are actually interested in flight training than 10,000 followers who could care less about aviation. The algorithms are getting really good at finding your target audiences and showing your content off to the appropriate people. So 100 views of a short you create from people interested in starting training in aviation is way better than 1,000 views of the same short from people who could care less about aviation.

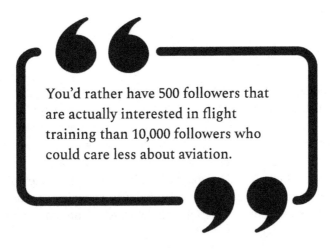

> You'd rather have 500 followers that are actually interested in flight training than 10,000 followers who could care less about aviation.

If you're just starting out, you don't need to go out and invest in a marketing agency or hire a marketing manager. Your front desk and CFIs can easily get this done for you. Furthermore, I don't recommend contracting this out to any marketing company. I'm a strong believer that social media needs to be handled by the business and not some third party. Keep it simple!

If you choose to hire a third party, you're going to be wasting a ton of time communicating back and forth with this company and they're also not going to be able to post genuine and authentic content. If the person posting on your social media is in-house, then you'll not only get the content uploaded faster, but in addition the content will appear genuine and real. Hire a marketing agency or "social media guru" and your posts and content will appear fake and spammy.

Social Media Flight Plan

The following is an outline of actionable steps you and your flight will take to create genuine and consistent content on your social media.

1. Create a business social media profile on all relevant social media networks (Facebook, Instagram, Youtube, Twitter, LinkedIn, and TikTok).
2. Link all of your social media profiles together.
3. Add links to your social media to your Google Business Profile and website.
4. Create a brand guide for your team members to follow. Outline your expectations for colors of overlays, fonts, usage of logo, etc.
5. Add all media assets (logo variations, overlays, etc.) to a shared folder for your team to access and use.
6. Commit to having you or your team post on all of your social media platforms at least once a week.
7. Respond to all comments on your own posts
8. Follow back and friend anyone who likes your page.
9. Respond to comments, like your students' posts, and engage with your audience.

Key Takeaways From Chapter 6

- Understand the differences of platforms and the type of demographics that spend their time on which platforms. TikTok and Instagram typically have a younger audience while Facebook and LinkedIn have an older audience.
- If you have not created a social media account for your flight school or personal use, create them.
- Create a YouTube account and add your videos there too. Make sure your videos add value and are of good quality.
- Post content on your personal profiles as well as business profiles. Your personal profile will have more leverage compared to your business profile typically. Use that to your advantage.
- When creating short-form video content, your goal is to "stop the scroll." Make sure you have a strong hook to get the viewer to stop scrolling.
- Be consistent and post as frequently as possible. The most ideal frequency is **daily**.
- Stay true to your message and branding. Regardless of the platform you are using, incorporate the same brand standards (logos, fonts, colors, and themes).
- Keep social media in-house and don't hire an agency to do your social media. Use CFIs and front desk team members to post your content before hiring a full-time or part-time marketing person at your school.
- Don't make a big deal of social media and number of likes of followers.

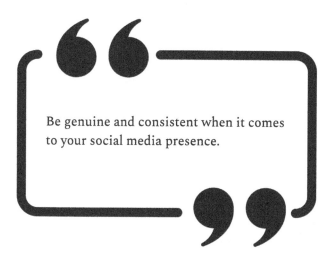

Be genuine and consistent when it comes to your social media presence.

Case Study In Social Media Marketing

Cirrus Aviation

Case in point, one of our previous clients, Cirrus Aviation, in Sarasota, Florida is a great example of consistent branding and messaging. Their brand is a bright lime green color with red accents and they emphasize professionalism and excellence. This is evident from the moment you walk in their door. Their walls are lime green and white and the staff greets you with a smile. In addition, their staff dons the same colors and their planes are painted the same colors too. On video calls with Nayda Cattin, the owner of Cirrus Aviation, she would always greet me with a smile while wearing a lime green scarf with a clean white button shirt embodying the brand and culture of her company.

Just this year, they passed their 30th year anniversary of being in business. They updated their logos and social media posts to include this celebration. While they changed a few things on their social media and website, they remained steadfast to their brand and culture. Recently, all of their social media posts have a lime green overlay placard showcasing their celebration of being 30 years in business.

Figure 6-2. Cirrus Aviation social media post picture with lime green painted plane and lime green overlay

AUGUST GROUND SCHOOL CALENDAR

Sunday	Monday	Tuesday	Wednesday	Thursday	Friday	Saturday
				1 Open Question IFR @1PM	2 Open Question VFR @1PM	3 Weather @6PM
4 W&B Aircraft Performance @6PM	5 Airspace @1PM	6 IFR Approach plates @1PM	7 Checkride Prep @6PM	8 Weather @6PM	9 Airport Operations @6PM	10 XC Planning @6PM
11 Open Question VFR @6PM	12 Aerodynamics @1PM	13 ADM @1PM	14 Airspace @6PM	15 Open Question IFR @6PM	16 Aeromedical @6PM	17 Systems @6PM
18 Open Question VFR @6PM	19	20 Open Question IFR @1PM	21 Checkride Prep @6PM	22 Weather @6PM	23 Open Question VFR @1PM	24 Open IFR @1PM
25 Open Question IR @6PM	26 W&B Aircraft Performance @6PM	27 Checkride Prep @6PM	28 XC Planning @6PM	29 Airport Operations @6PM	30 Systems @1PM	31 Open Question VFR @6PM

Call or Text 941-360-9074 to signup, or Email Dispatch@Cirrusaviation.com

Make sure to sign up at least 24 hrs in advance as classes are confirmed on attendance.

Figure 6-3. Cirrus Aviation social media post of event calendar

In addition to having consistent branding, they also regularly post updates regarding checkride passes, solos, and events on their social media. They even have a calendar they share to the world where they let everyone know when their upcoming events will be.

Cirrus Aviation does a great job of keeping people in the loop. They regularly post on social media about what's happening at the flight school. Whether it's a student passing their checkride, a pilot going solo for the first time, or a big event coming up, they make sure everyone knows about it. They also share pictures and videos that show their bright lime green planes and the school's facilities. By doing this, Cirrus Aviation not only informs their audience but also keeps them excited about flying.

The success of Cirrus Aviation's social media efforts shows how important it is to be active online. They have built a strong community by regularly updating their social media pages and sharing quality content. Your flight school can learn from Cirrus Aviation's approach of staying true to their brand, using great visuals, and posting often. Keep it simple, share real stories, and use social media smartly to help your flight school connect with more people and attract new students.

Email Marketing For Flight Schools

Chapter 7

The past chapters have been about creating positioning assets to create the best authority for your flight school business. This starts with your website and making sure that you have properly set up appropriate calls to actions and provide multiple methods for prospects to reach you. Then we optimize the website using on-page SEO and then start creating links through directory listings, partnerships, your GMB profile, and social media profiles (off-page SEO and reputation management). These are all tactics to push the needle forward with inbound leads - prospects that contact you directly for your services.

This chapter is going to be a bit different as this marketing tactic requires you to do a bit of outreach. Email marketing is a powerful tool for connecting with your prospects and maintaining relationships with your current students. By using strategic email campaigns, you can keep your audience informed, engaged, and excited about what your flight school has to offer. It's all about being "omnipresent" in your target customer's life - whether or not they are a paying customer or prospect. You want to always be top of mind and be regarded as the best place for flight training.

We will cover several important aspects of email marketing, starting with the basics of setting up a professional email domain to ensure your emails look credible and trustworthy. From there, we'll dive into specific campaigns like 5-star review requests, database reactivation, and automated emails for discovery flights.

You'll also learn how to craft effective transactional emails for form submissions and create nurture sequences that guide your prospects through the enrollment process. Additionally, we will explore the importance of newsletters and how to use them to share success stories, announcements, and upcoming events with your audience.

By the end of this chapter, you'll have a comprehensive understanding of how to leverage email marketing to boost your flight school's visibility, credibility, and student enrollment.

Setting Up The Infrastructure

Before you start your email marketing campaigns, it's essential to set up the proper infrastructure. This involves getting a separate domain for email sending and choosing the right software for your email marketing needs.

Getting Another Domain for Email Sending

Using a separate domain for email sending helps maintain your main domain's reputation and ensures that your emails reach your audience's inbox. For example, if your main website is "YourFlightSchool.com," consider getting a domain like "YourFlightSchoolMail.com" or "YourFlightSchool.net" for email marketing purposes. This domain will be used exclusively for sending marketing emails, which can help you avoid deliverability issues and protect your primary domain from being flagged as spam.

If you have a high bounce rate or a high spam rate on your primary domain, then that can kill your SEO progress and also affect email sending for non-marketing purposes.

Setting up a separate domain is pretty straightforward:

1. Choose a domain that is related to your main business name.
2. Purchase the domain through a reliable domain registrar.
3. Configure the domain's DNS settings to point to your email marketing service provider.

Software for Email Marketing

There are many different options you can choose from to implement your email marketing strategy. The software you choose should offer features like automation, analytics, and template customization. Here are a few popular options:

- **Flight School CRM**: This is the CRM (customer relationship management) software that we give for free to our flight school partners. It has features which allow for email automation and email marketing campaigns. We'll get more into this in Chapter 9.
- **Mailchimp**: Known for its user friendly interface and robust features, Mailchimp is great for beginners and offers a variety of templates and automation tools.
- **Constant Contact**: This platform is excellent for small businesses, offering powerful email marketing tools and easy to use templates.

- **Other CRM Software**: Tools like Infusionsoft, Keap, Monday, and Salesforce also have features to do email marketing.

Once you have selected your email marketing software, take the time to set up your account properly. Import your email list, create groups or tags based on different criteria (such as leads, current students, and alumni), and design your email templates to match your branding. Make sure to also configure your email authentication settings (SPF, DKIM, and DMARC) to improve deliverability and protect your domain from being spoofed.

By setting up a dedicated domain and choosing the right software, you lay a strong foundation for successful email marketing campaigns that will help grow your flight school business.

Campaign Implementation Process

In this section, we will explore some proven email campaigns that we've seen benefit our flight schools. Each of these campaigns serves a unique purpose and can help you achieve different marketing goals, from re-engaging past leads to gathering positive reviews and guiding prospects through the enrollment process.

Database Reactivation

This is a great place to start if you are a flight school that has been established for a few years and you have not done email marketing in the past. Even still, if you are a new flight school or have done email marketing already there might be a few pointers that you can pick up from this section that can help with your current practices.

The main idea of a database reactivation campaign is to send an email to people that have previously interacted with your business but did not end up pursuing pilot training.

Gather the List

Step one is building a list and making sure that it is high quality. What we mean by building a list is preparing email addresses of contacts that have interacted with your business. These email addresses should be valid and real. If you send mass email out and it has a high bounce rate or errors on sending due to incorrect addresses, this will diminish the reputation of your domain and pretty soon your emails will start to land in the spam folder.

Make sure to scrape every possible source you may have. Start with your website leads. Anyone that has filled out a contact form will have provided you with their email. Next, look at other places to scrape. Maybe you had a newsletter sign up form built into your website, or maybe you had a booth at a local event (job fairs, educational career fairs, aviation events, airport events, etc.) where you had visitors give you their contact information.

Lastly, include past students that no longer fly at your school or people that might have booked a discovery flight but did not pursue pilot training should be also added to the list. Remove current students from the list as we will be targeting these people as prospects to re-engage with you. Certainly, a majority of these people will not take any action, but there will be a percentage that will respond. In addition, if the prospect is to ever think about flight training again, you will be first considered. Finally after you have a clean and compiled list of prospects, you will send them a sequence of emails for the next few months.

Main Email Format

Creating a marketing email is simple and you don't need to overthink it. The main formula is

- **Be genuine and authentic.** Try not to make the email sound robotic or that it's been sent to countless numbers of people.
- **Emphasize the benefits of flight training.** Usually this entails focusing on career opportunities and improving your students lives.
- **Highlight your authority.** Include small cues to show off your authority and position yourself as the best.
- **Make a limited time offer.** A sales tactic that many expert salesmen and marketers use is to create artificial scarcity. Give them a limited time offer, or restrict the number of seats available. People love FOMO (fear of missing out) and it's a great motivator.
- **End with a call to action.** Give the reader a task to complete. Whether that's calling you or filling out a form, make sure the reader knows what the next steps are.

Below are some ideas that we've used in the past for our flight schools that have helped bring in new students that were thought to have been tire kickers or visitors that were simply not interested in flight training. If you couple these customized emails along with retargeting ads (we'll get into this in Chapter 8), you'll increase your chances of enrolling more students.

Group Ground School Invitation

{{First Name}},

Thank you for your interest in **{{Flight School Name}}**. As an Air Force veteran owned flight school family business, we extend our gratitude to you and invite you to become part of our aviation family.

If you're just starting out in your aviation journey, you might be wondering where to start. You're not alone. Many aspiring pilots get lost in the sea of information and feel discouraged by the high costs of flight training.

But getting started doesn't take much. All you need is a commitment to learn and an open mind. That's why we created the **Private Pilot Group Ground School Course** to help you take your first steps towards obtaining your wings. It's an affordable way to join the aviation community at {{Airport Name}} and get your first endorsement in your logbook.

For a limited time, you can enroll in our group ground school for only $500. You'll join a group of aspiring pilots just like you. You'll learn aeronautical fundamentals, regulations, weather flight planning, and more. By the end of the course, you'll have an endorsement from one of our instructors to take the FAA written exam.

We guarantee you'll ace the exam. Completing the written exam before any flight training will position you to excel in your flight training, and you'll have your private pilot certificate in no time!

Call us or fill out the form below to get started. We look forward to meeting you and helping you crush your aviation goals.

Enroll Now: ({{Link to Form}})
Call us at: {{Flight School Phone Number}}

New Airplane Email

{{First Name}},

We're thrilled to announce that we've expanded our multi-engine fleet, providing better availability for multi-engine training. With more aircraft and resources, {{Flight School Name}} is now better equipped to help you achieve your aviation goals.

Why Get A Multi-Engine Rating?

- **Competitive Edge:** Having a multi-engine rating and flight hours makes your resume stand out in the pilot job market.
- **Skill Expansion:** Whether you're expanding your skills or pursuing a career in aviation, we can help you succeed.

Our Proven Track Record
Our successful graduates speak for themselves. As a leading flight school in {{Local Area}}, we are excited to offer this new training program. With our new Piper Twin Engine Seminole, you'll train on modern, well maintained aircraft to gain true proficiency in multi-engine operations.

Join Our Aviation Family
Come check us out and say hello! We're happy to welcome you to our aviation family. Call us at {{Phone Number}} or visit our website at {{Website Address}} to get started.

Learn More About Our Multi-Engine Training
{{Website Address}}

Sincerely,
{{Owner Name}}

Open House Invitation

{{First Name}},

We noticed you showed interest in our flight school but haven't taken the next step yet. We understand that choosing the right flight school is a big decision, so we want to invite you to our upcoming Open House event on {{event date}}.

Why Attend Our Open House?

- **Explore Our Facilities:** Take a guided tour of our state-of-the-art training facilities and see where you'll be learning to fly.
- **Meet Our Instructors:** Get to know our experienced, friendly instructors who will answer any questions you have about flight training.
- **Discover Our Fleet:** Check out our well-maintained aircraft and learn about the different types of planes you'll be flying.
- **Special Offers:** Exclusive discounts and promotions for attendees who enroll in our programs during the event.

Event Details:
- **Date:** {{event date}}
- **Time:** {{Event Start Time}} to {{Event End Time}}

- **Location:** {{Flight School Address}}
- **RSVP:** Please let us know if you can make it by {{RSVP Deadline}}. You can RSVP by calling us at {{Phone Number}} or clicking the link below.

RSVP Now!! {{RSVP Link}}

This is a perfect opportunity to get a firsthand look at what flight training is all about and to ask any questions you might have. We're confident that once you see what we have to offer, you'll be excited to join our aviation family.

Don't miss out on this chance to explore your future in aviation. We look forward to seeing you at our Open House event on {{event date}}!

Sincerely,
{{Owner Name}}
{{Flight School Name}}
{{Phone Number}}
Visit Our Website {{Website Address}}

5 Star Review Campaign

The next email campaign we are going to talk about is called the 5 star review campaign. As mentioned in Chapter 5, having a plethora of 5 star reviews with details and pictures on your Google Business profile helps build your flight school's reputation and attract new students. Positive reviews can greatly influence potential students' decisions and help them trust your school. By asking for 5 star reviews, you can make sure your flight school stands out.

Reviews are like word of mouth recommendations, but online, where everyone can see them. The more positive reviews you have, the better your school will look to people searching for flight training.

From what I've seen, most flight schools have on average around 20 or so reviews, with flight schools that have not made marketing a priority stay in the teens or even single digits. On the other hand, there are other schools that are more established and have made efforts in their marketing to push out more than 50 reviews, or even more than 100 reviews in their Google Business Profile.

Positive reviews improve your flight school's online presence. Good ratings and feedback on sites like Google and Yelp can make it easier for people to find you. When your school has lots of good reviews, it also shows up higher in search results, so more people will see it. Not only does it look good on your reputation, but you get better search rankings as well!

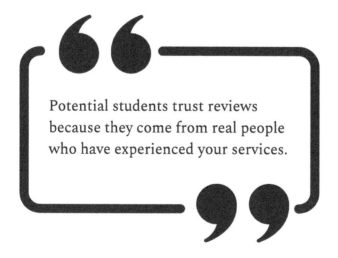

> Potential students trust reviews because they come from real people who have experienced your services.

Whom To Target

Focus on students who had good experiences at your flight school. This includes recent graduates who finished their training and students who have soloed or reached big milestones. Also target students who have given you good feedback in person or through surveys. Long term students who are loyal and happy with your school are also great candidates for reviews. By targeting these groups, you can ensure that the reviews you get are positive and genuine.

You typically don't want to send this email to students that have just started training at your school, and you especially don't want to send this to students that have washed out, failed stagechecks or checkrides, or students who have taken on large amounts of debt. You might get some negative reviews bundled in there inadvertently if you don't tailor and filter your list.

Implementation Plan

There are five easy steps to successfully launch your 5 star review campaign. At Right Rudder Marketing, we've seen flight schools go from less than 20 reviews to over 50 in less than 6 months by following these steps:

1. **Identify Satisfied Students:**
   Look at your student records and feedback to find those who had positive experiences. Check for students who have recently completed their training or reached significant milestones like first solos.

2. **Craft a Friendly Request:**
   Send a personalized email thanking them and asking for a review. Be sincere and to the point. Make sure to mention how much their feedback means to you

and how it helps other students.

3. **Provide Easy Links:**
   Include direct links to your review pages on Google, Yelp, and other sites to make it easy for them. The simpler it is for them to leave a review, the more likely they are to do it.

4. **Offer Incentives (optional):**
   Offer a small incentive like a discount on items in your pilot shop or their next lesson or even giving a free ground school session to encourage new reviews. Make sure the incentive is something they will find valuable.

5. **Follow Up and Keep Trying**
   If they don't respond, send a polite reminder after a week or two. In addition, have placards or QR codes on the front desk linking to the review page. You can even add the link to the bottom of your or your CFI's email signature. You can also approach this via SMS texting or via social media DMs instead of emails.

Email Template

```
Dear current and former {{Flight School Name}}
students,

I'm reaching out today to ask for your support in
helping spread the word about our excellent flight
training program. As a small, locally owned
business, positive online reviews are incredibly
important for attracting new students and allowing
us to continue operating successfully.
```

If you had a great experience learning to fly with us, it would mean so much if you could take a couple of minutes to leave a 5-star review for {{Flight School Name}} on Google Maps.

Online reviews provide valuable feedback and social proof that helps prospective students feel confident in choosing us for their pilot training.

Leaving a review is quick and easy. Simply visit the link below for our Google listing, click 5 stars, and let others know about the top notch instruction and aircraft you received at {{Flight School Name}}.

{{Link To Review Page}}

Each 5-star review helps our flight school immensely and allows us to keep offering best-in-class pilot training for aviators in the greater {{City Name}} area. We're so grateful for your support!

Best,

{{Owner Name}}

Automated Sequences To Enhance Operations

The next set of emails we're going to look at are emails not focused on marketing and sales, but rather email automations you can build out to enhance your operations. How many hours per month does your front desk or administrative staff take sending the same emails? These can include:

- Pricing Inquiries
- Discovery flight FAQs

- Post discovery flight enrollment follow ups
- New student onboarding instructions

The most basic implementation you can have ready in your pocket is to draft these emails as a template and have your administrative staff send them as required. Save them in a word document and have them be readily accessible to your relevant team members.

A more advanced version of this is to use software to set up specific triggers in your CRM or website. If you are using WordPress, there are certain plugins like WPForms that you can configure to send specific emails based on visitor responses to forms. On the other hand, if you are using a CRM you can stream the form data from your website to the CRM and then build out automations that filter based on certain responses.

For new student onboarding, if you are using a CRM and have built out a funnel or a pipeline to track your leads progress in the sales process, then you can build the trigger based on when you mark the lead as "won" or "complete." We'll get into more specifics about how to configure your CRM in Chapter 9.

I won't provide templates this time around because every flight school is different and may have a certain twist or variation to these emails, but the idea is the same. Have these emails ready to respond to your prospects and future student pilots.

In Figure 7-1 on page 7-17, I visually explain how these workflows should be created for a discovery flight booking. The automation workflow starts when a discovery flight form is submitted. This gets the lead into your pipeline and then activates the automation sequence.

If the lead makes it all the way through and responds positively, then this would then activate the new student onboarding process where you might send an email talking about what to expand on day one of flight school, have a PDF describing your flight school training program, and also solicit the new student to submit documents for TSA verification and insurance, and lastly informing them to review, sign, and return your renters agreement and student policy.

If you have not invested in email sending tools or CRM software, I think it's important to highlight that you want to give your team members the resources and tools they need to be successful at their jobs.

Start out slow and do things manually at first. You can easily register a new domain and email account to start things off. As mentioned before, have the email templates in a shared folder so you and your team members can send consistent emails with the same information and messaging.

And then eventually when you uncover the deficiencies in your processes, find the right software tools to fix the issues and save you and your team time. It's like flight planning with charts and a plotter and then moving on to using an EFB. Get the fundamentals down first and then the shortcuts to start saving your team time which will increase your bottom line and save you money.

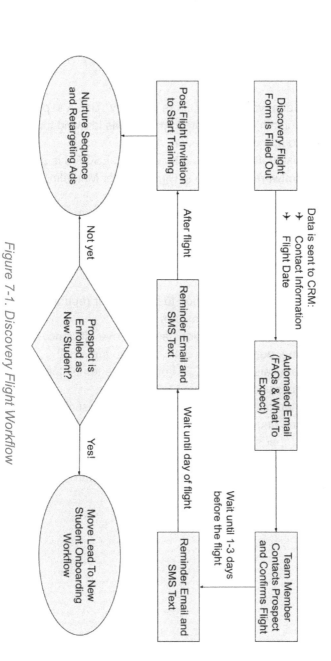

Figure 7-1. Discovery Flight Workflow

Key Takeaways From Chapter 7

- Setup your infrastructure correctly. Use a separate domain for automated email sends to avoid tarnishing your domain reputation.
- Use software to send bulk email. FSCRM is a free software tool given to Right Rudder Marketing flight schools.
- Regardless of whatever email campaign and tools you use, make sure that your lists are filtered and clean.
- Make sure that the email message makes sense for the recipient.
- Use email automation to bolster your reputation in regards to online reviews.
- To enhance operations and improve efficiency with your administrative staff, program the email templates in your CRM or have the templates readily accessible in a shared folder.
- Map out your workflow and process visually so that you and your team members understand what the proper steps are.
- Start things off manually and then once you have established processes, invest in software and tools to save money and time.

> Give the proper tools to your team members for them to be successful at their jobs.

Advertising Online With Pay Per Click

Chapter 8

PPC, or pay per click is the most popular form of online advertising as of today. Simply put, PPC means that you put an ad out into the internet, most popularly Google, and you pay whenever someone clicks on your ad. PPC allows you to target specific audiences and demographics. This means you can reach potential students who are actively searching for flight training and are more likely to enroll.

In this chapter, we will explore the basics of PPC advertising, how to set up your campaigns, and the best practices for managing and optimizing them. You will learn how to choose the right keywords, create compelling ads, and set budgets that align with your marketing goals. We will also discuss tracking and analyzing your campaign performance to ensure you are getting the best results possible.

Whether you are new to PPC advertising or looking to improve your current efforts, this chapter will provide you with the knowledge you need to succeed. With a well executed PPC strategy, your flight school can reach more prospective students and achieve steady consistent growth. Paired with a good website and SEO, this combo is the main meat and potatoes of how to market your flight school business online.

Why Invest in Online Advertising?

SEO, email marketing, and social social media can be thought of as a slow organic process. While it can pay the highest dividends in your overall marketing strategy, it can take several months before you see some real traction and your efforts bear fruit.

On the other hand, running an advertising campaign can quickly accelerate your efforts and you can start to see new leads come in within the first month. In addition, running an advertising campaign online means that you'll get access to each platform's tools and features. You'll be able to target specific demographics and keywords. You'll also receive analytic data to see how your campaigns are performing, and then tweak your campaigns accordingly. Lastly, you can scale up or down as you want. If you want to enroll five new students this month, then you can increase your ad spend and create new ad copy and ad groups. If your staff are overloaded and planes fully booked, then you can simply lower your budget or pause your campaigns.

Another thing to note about PPC advertising is that it also benefits your SEO and organic rankings. As more people visit your website, Google will bring you up higher in the rankings.

What's A Good Budget?

I think the main thing I want to say in regards to this is that there is a MOQ (minimum order quantity). While not enforced, if you do not spend a certain amount of money, you will not see a good return on your investment and you will actually end up wasting money. A good ballpark estimate is that you should be spending at least $1000 a month on online ads.

Even further, when you start spending more than $5000 a month, the CPC (cost per click) will be a bit less and your ROAS (return on ad spend) will be significantly higher. That being said, most flight schools Right Rudder Marketing works with spend between $1000 and $2000 a month on PPC ads, specifically Google ads.

To put this in perspective, at $1000 a month that's about $33 per day budgeted. Your daily ad spend will vary day to day based on how many people click your ads. As of the writing of this book (summer / fall of 2024), in most markets the CPC (cost per click) hovers around $5 to $10 per click. At $7 per click, you're going to see around four people per day clicking your ad which equates to a little over 100 clicks per month. Out of those 100 clicks, about ten visitors will fill out a form or engage with your business and become a lead. Most sales teams average around a 20% close ratio, so you should expect to see around two new student pilots enrolled in your flight school per month when you spend $1000.

Considering the LTV (lifetime value) of flight school customers which on average sits at around $10,000, you can potentially make around $20,000 for the $1000 you spend which is a great return.

However, to get these returns you really need to dial in your processes and put in the right work to see these numbers. If you simply throw money at Google and don't optimize anything and think Google will do all the work for you, you're unfortunately mistaken. Google will gladly spend your ad budget and if you aren't careful, you won't see the results you're after. Don't fill out their forms (simple mode) and let them create and manage the campaign for you. The Google Ads signup form is specifically engineered to extract as much money from you as possible by putting your campaign on autopilot and it is in your best interest to learn how to advertise online the right way and do it manually.

We're going to explain how you can run your ad campaigns the right way. We'll start with some core concepts first. This is important because these concepts can be applied to any PPC platform. We'll then get into the details with Google ads and Facebook/Instagram ads as they are the most popular choices and also have the most number of users. Therefore, those platforms provide the most possible potential leads. Bing, Reddit, and Yelp are also good platforms, but I wouldn't recommend investing in those platforms if you haven't done Google and Meta ads first.

PPC Basics

As we touched on earlier, PPC which stands for pay per click advertising, is an online marketing model where you pay a fee each time your ad is clicked. It's a way to buy visits to your site rather than earning them organically. For flight schools, PPC can be a powerful tool to attract prospective students who are actively searching for flight training programs. By targeting specific keywords related to aviation and flight training, your ads can appear at the top of search engine results pages (SERPs), making it easier for interested individuals to find your school.

When you create a PPC ad, you bid on specific keywords that you believe potential students might use when searching for flight training. Your ad competes with other advertisers bidding on the same keywords. The search engine then uses a combination of your bid amount and the quality of your ad (measured by a quality score) to determine the ad's placement on the SERP. This system ensures that users see relevant, high-quality ads related to their search queries.

Click Through Rate

CTR is the percentage of people who click your ad after seeing it, indicating how well your ad resonates with viewers. Let's say your ad campaign has 2000 impressions in a month. And out of those 2000 impressions, 200 people clicked on your ad. Then in that case your CTR is 10%. In Figure 8-2, I provide a recent example of one of our flight schools achieving a 10% CTR. However, this is not the norm. In 2024 the average CTR for Google Ads in the educational sector was 6.42% among 17,000 US-based Google ad campaigns[17].

$$CTR = \frac{Total\ Clicks\ On\ Your\ Ad}{Total\ Ad\ Impressions}$$

Figure 8-1. Click through rate equation

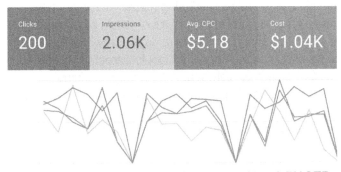

Figure 8-2. Google ad performance with a 9.7%CTR

Cost Per Click

CPC is the amount you pay each time someone clicks on your ad, which can vary based on the competition for your chosen keywords. Quality score is a metric used by search engines to evaluate the relevance and quality of your ads and landing pages. A higher quality score can lead to better ad placements and lower CPCs. Having a well structured SEO website paired with relevant ads and keywords will yield a better quality score and lower CPC.

In addition to the quality score, the CPC is also determined by the immediate market, more specifically your geographical location and also other businesses that are competing for similar sets of keywords. For example, back in 2022 the average CPC that I was seeing firsthand was around $7 to $9. Fast forward to mid-2024, I am now seeing CPC hovering around $5 to $7. It's actually gotten a bit cheaper to run ads. However, the market is always volatile and can fluctuate depending on external factors.

If a new flight school at your airport pops up and starts running an aggressive marketing campaign and invests heavily in PPC advertising, you're going to have a competitor bidding for the same keywords you are and in tandem, the CPC is going to increase.

We see this first hand when I work with schools that have an ATP Flight School in their area. ATP Flight School invests heavily in their online marketing and have good footholds in the bidding market for relevant flight school keywords. These flight school's CPC is usually much higher compared to flight schools that are not near an ATP Flight School.

When Google Adwords (the previous name for Google Ads) was first introduced in 2000 they did not do PPC or CPC. Their initial model was actually pay per impression. They moved to the PPC model in 2002 to make Google Ads more accessible to a variety of businesses. And at that time, the CPC was lower than a dollar per click and just a mere few pennies[18]. Times sure have changed since then and now Google Ads brings in billions of dollars of revenue for the monolithic search engine company.

Conversions

Another term that gets thrown around when talking about PPC advertising is conversions. A conversion occurs when a user takes a desired action after clicking your ad. This action could be filling out a form, signing up for a newsletter, booking a discovery flight, giving you a call, or even enrolling in a flight training program. Tracking conversions allows you to measure the effectiveness of your PPC campaigns and understand which ads are driving the most valuable actions.

To track conversions, you need to set up conversion tracking in your PPC platform. For Google Ads, this involves placing a conversion tracking tag or code onto your website. This tag tracks your website's users then records when they complete a specific action like submitting a form. By analyzing this data, you can see which keywords, ads, and landing pages are driving the most conversions.

For our flight school clients, we consider a conversion from a PPC ad to be a lead. This is because this person has given you their contact information like their email address and phone number.

The number of conversions depends on the number of clicks and impressions you get, your reputation and brand image, and how well you structure your website and social media to convert for sales.

Algorithms and Automatic Adjustments

A thing to note about ads is that Google, Meta, or any other advertising platform will always try to spend your money. If you are experiencing a low amount of clicks, then they might try increasing impressions. On the other hand, if you're getting lots of clicks, they will lower the amount of impressions.

This can have a drastic effect on conversions. For search ads, which is the primary version of Google and Bing ads where your ads show up on search results, we do not pay for conversions or leads. We only pay for each click. PPC platforms like Google do not really care if you got a conversion or lead. They only care if the ad was clicked because each click is several dollars in their pockets. This being said, a low CTR is not necessarily a bad thing if you have high impressions and high conversions.

> Google, Meta, or any other advertising platform will always try to spend your money.

Components of an Advertisement

To keep it simple there are only two main key components when it comes to creating an ad:

- ✈ Ad copy
- ✈ Targeting

Each of one of these elements plays a role in ensuring your ad reaches the right audience and compels them to take action. Let's break down these components in detail.

Ad Copy

Ad copy is the text of your advertisement. In this category, I'm also including the pictures and videos that might be included in your ad depending on the type of ad you are running. Your ad copy needs to be compelling and encourage viewers to take action.

For flight schools, the ad copy should highlight the benefits of your programs and address potential students' pain points. Use strong calls to action, such as "Become an Airline Pilot Today and Learn To Fly" or "Take the First Step: Book Your Discovery Flight Now."

Your ad copy should also include keywords that your target audience is likely to use when searching for flight training. This not only helps your ad appear in relevant searches but also resonates with the searchers' intent.

When writing ad copy, it's important to focus on what sets your flight school apart from the competition. Mention unique selling points like experienced instructors, modern aircraft, or flexible scheduling. Testimonials or success stories can also be powerful in convincing prospective students. Remember, your goal is to grab attention quickly and make it clear why someone should choose your flight school.

If you're using video ads on Facebook or YouTube, you're going to want to make sure your ads are captivating and keep the user interested enough to not click off the ad and skip the video.

- **Create the hook** - The first three seconds of the video are the most important part of your video ad. Your ad should be intriguing by addressing concerns or evoking emotions. Stop the scroll or stop them from clicking off.
- **Make the audience know it's for them** - If you're targeting highschool students and their parents in Chicago, Illinois then you might start your video ad with, "If you're a teenager in Chicagoland thinking about flying..."
- **Don't forget the CTA** - Always end with a call to action and ways for the viewer to contact you. Give your offer and outline the steps needed to get started.

Targeting

Targeting ensures that your ads are shown to the right people. This involves several factors including demographics, keywords, location, and more. By refining your targeting, you can reach potential students who are most likely to be interested in your flight training programs.

- **Demographics** - Demographic targeting allows you to narrow down your audience based on age, gender, income, education level, and more. For example, if you know that most of your students are young adults interested in a career in aviation, you can target that specific age group. For Facebook Meta ads, you can

target people that are members in certain groups or following certain pages.
- **Keywords** - Keywords are the terms that people type into search engines when looking for information. Choosing the right keywords is essential for getting your ads in front of the right audience. Use keyword research tools to find popular search terms related to flight training. Long tail keywords, which are more specific phrases, can often be more effective because they target users who are closer to making a decision. While long tail keywords have a lower search volume, it also has less competition and oftentimes has lower CPC.
- **Location** - Location targeting ensures your ads are seen by people in specific geographic areas. For flight schools, this is especially important because most students will be looking for training programs near them. You can target ads to people within a certain radius of your flight school or within specific cities or regions. On the other hand, if your flight school is located outside a major city, you can use location based targeting to bring in students from the major city into your flight school.
- **Negative Keywords** - Negative keywords are terms you specify to prevent your ads from being shown to irrelevant searchers. For example, if you offer flight training but not drone piloting courses, you might use "drone" as a negative keyword. This ensures that people searching for drone training won't see your ads, saving you money and improving the relevance of your ad impressions.

By carefully crafting your ad copy and strategically targeting your audience, you can create effective PPC advertisements that attract potential students and drive enrollments in your flight training programs.

Now, let's get into the different forms of online advertising and some of the various platforms available. If you have the basics of how advertising works, then it really doesn't matter what platform you use or what type of ads you are running. The concepts described above will be used in all platforms and types of ads.

Types of Online Ads

Search Ads

Search ads are one of the most common and effective forms of online advertising for flight schools. These ads appear at the top of search engine results pages when users type in relevant keywords related to flight training. Search ads are typically marked as "sponsored" or "ad," but because they appear alongside organic search results, they can still attract a lot of attention and clicks.

I really recommend this form of advertising because they target people who are already actively searching for flight training or related services. When someone types in keywords like "flight schools near me" or "learn to fly," they're showing clear intent and interest in what your flight school offers. This makes them a warmer lead compared to someone who might come across your ad on Facebook or through a display ad (which we'll get to later), where they weren't necessarily looking for flight training at that moment.

Unlike social media ads, where you're often trying to grab the attention of users who may not have considered flight training, search ads reach people at the moment they are most likely to take action. These potential students are already in the mindset of exploring their options, so when they see your ad at the top of the search results, they're more likely to click through and engage with your content. This leads to higher conversion rates because you're connecting with people who are further along in the decision making process.

In contrast, with Facebook ads or display ads, you're often casting a wider net to catch the interest of a broader audience, many of whom may not be actively looking for flight training. While these ads have their place in raising awareness and building your brand, search ads give you the advantage of targeting people who are already primed to take the next step toward enrolling in your programs. By focusing on search ads, you can efficiently allocate your marketing budget to reach leads who are more likely to convert into paying students.

Google Ads is the most popular platform for search ads, allowing you to bid on keywords that your potential students might be searching for. When someone searches for terms like "flight school near me" or "pilot training programs," your ad can appear at the top of the results, giving you prime visibility. Google's vast reach and advanced targeting options make it a powerful tool for reaching a wide audience, whether they're searching on a desktop or mobile device.

Bing Ads, though less popular than Google, should not be overlooked. Bing holds a decent share of the search market, especially among certain demographics like older and senior consumers. Running search ads on Bing can be a cost-effective way to reach users who might not be searching on Google. Often, the competition for keywords is lower on

Bing, which can result in a lower cost per click (CPC) and better return on investment (ROI).

Search Engine Market Share

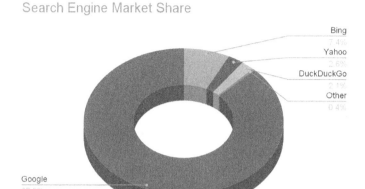

Figure 8-3. Search engine market share[19]

Search ads work by targeting specific keywords that are relevant to your flight school. You bid on these keywords, and your ad is displayed when someone searches for them. The goal is to match your ad with the intent of the searcher, making it more likely that they will click on your ad and take action, such as visiting your website or filling out a contact form.

Display Ads

These ads appear on websites that are part of Google's Display Network allowing you to reach potential students as they browse the web. Unlike search ads, which target users actively searching for flight training and show up on search results, display ads show up on various websites on the internet.

Google's Performance Max, a form of display ads, uses machine learning to optimize your ad placements across multiple channels, including YouTube, Gmail, Search, and the Display Network. Performance Max campaigns allow you to reach potential students at various stages of their journey, using different formats and messages tailored to their behavior. This can help you maximize your reach and efficiency by targeting users who are more likely to convert, based on Google's vast amount of user data.

While display ads might not drive conversions as directly as search ads, they still play a role in your overall marketing strategy by keeping your flight school in front of a wide audience. When used in conjunction with other ad types, such as search and video ads, display ads can help create a comprehensive marketing approach that nurtures leads from initial awareness to final conversion.

Video Ads

YouTube is the second largest search engine after Google, making it an ideal platform for running video ads. People often turn to YouTube for tutorials, reviews, and educational content, which aligns perfectly with the interests of aspiring pilots. Even outside of doing advertisements, you should create a YouTube channel for your school as that helps with SEO, increases your authority, and if people see your ad they will usually check out your YouTube channel as a next step.

You can target your video ads based on keywords, demographics, and even the types of videos your potential students are watching. For example, if someone is watching a video about the best flight schools or how to get a pilot's license, your ad can appear before or during the video, directly reaching a warm audience that is already interested in aviation.

Facebook and Instagram are also effective platforms for video advertising, especially for reaching a younger audience. These platforms allow you to target users based on their interests, behaviors, and demographic information. Since Facebook and Instagram are more social and visually driven, short, engaging video content works best. For instance, a 30-second video showcasing a day in the life of a flight student or a quick tour of your facilities can capture the viewer's interest and drive them to learn more about your school.

The advantage of video ads on Facebook and Instagram is their ability to appear seamlessly within the user's feed, stories, or reels, making them less intrusive while still being highly visible. These ads are often more engaging than traditional banner display ads or search ads because they can tell a story and evoke emotions, which can be particularly effective in the aviation industry where the thrill of flying is a strong emotional pull.

Incorporating video ads into your marketing strategy allows you to connect with potential students on a deeper level, showing them not just what your school offers, but also why they should choose you. While video creation is a resource intensive process, it's a marketing tool that pays dividends. Start a YouTube channel, post on social media, and run ads to reach new audiences.

LSA Ads

Recently, Google has been pushing a new form of advertising called LSA ads, or local search ads. This is a pay per lead model where you would pay for each conversion which is different from PPC or pay per click.

In this case, you will only pay whenever someone clicks the ad and fills out a form or gives you a call. Since we're paying per lead and not per click, the cost is going to be significantly higher. As of the writing of this book, LSA ads are not available for the flight school industry but we may see some changes in the near future. These types of ads may eventually take over search ads as Google is pushing this hard in other industries. This is because each lead can cost $150 to $300 instead of just $5 per click. A majority of our flight schools see around $50 to $100 per lead using the search ad method so I personally hope they delay rolling this out to our industry. However, the change is inevitable and it's worth knowing about it and keeping an eye on future changes at Google.

Lead Generation Ads

Lead generation ads are specifically designed to capture contact information from potential students directly within the platform, without requiring them to leave and visit your website. These ads are commonly found on social media platforms like Facebook, Instagram, and LinkedIn. These ads show up on users' feeds where they can quickly fill out a form with just a few taps or clicks.

Another advantage of lead generation ads is that they allow you to collect valuable information about your prospects right from the start. You can tailor your forms to ask specific questions, such as what stage they are in their flight training journey or what type of pilot license they are interested in pursuing. This data can help you segment your audience and create more personalized follow up campaigns.

These formats allow you to reach potential students who are already engaging with aviation related content, making your ads more relevant and effective. By adding lead generation ads into your overall marketing strategy, you can streamline the process of converting prospects into students and keep your sales pipeline full.

Retargeting Ads

Since we're already talking about ads on social media, it's worth mentioning a special type of social media ad called a retargeting ad.

In this type of ad, you're going to upload your list of leads to Meta ad manager and create a new audience. Then you show your ads to only this audience. In addition, if you install the Meta Pixel into your website, any new website visitors will also be shown the ad and will be added to your custom audience. This helps convert lost leads and folks that were on the fence about flight training. It's a very powerful and effective tool to stay omnipresent in your target customers' minds.

Your Next Steps

This chapter went over the foundations of how online advertising works. There are many types of ads out there and various platforms that you can use, but the fundamentals stay the same: What is your ad copy, and who is your target.

We also went over some of the main data drivers you're going to want to look at when running your ads: CTR, CPC, and conversions.

To run an effective ad campaign, you should be reviewing your numbers monthly. The main numbers we focus on at Right Rudder Marketing when we look at flight school ad performance is conversions and cost per lead.

Look at how many conversions you got in a month and how much you spent. At the end of the day, what really matters is did you enroll more students in your flight school? If you aren't seeing as many conversions as you like, then review the fundamentals. Are you targeting your ideal customer? Does your message actually resonate with that ideal customer?

Create The Ad Manager Account

If you haven't already created the account, create the account and get started. Set a budget and start running the ads. Hopefully, after reading this chapter you understand more of what each setting and option means.

Make sure you don't let the platform run on autopilot. It's specifically engineered to take your money. For Google Ads, that means veering away from Google's Smart Mode and activating Expert Mode. For Meta Ads, that means no longer boosting a post and instead, creating a campaign and configuring the correct audiences.

Track and Measure

Once the ads start rolling the last piece of the puzzle is to track and measure. Run multiple campaigns and/or ad groups and see which ones have the most engagement.

Scale those ads with more budget and scale back the ads that are not seeing the same amount of attention. That way you maximize the effectiveness of your budget.

Last but not least, don't set it and forget it. Running online advertising campaigns is a continuous process. Make sure that you're reviewing your data constantly and making sure that your money is being spent wisely. Additionally, nothing lasts forever. Ad copy runs stale after 3-6 months and if it's shown to the same audience, it runs stale even quicker. Refresh your settings, come up with new creative ads and media, and play around with your audiences and targets.

Key Takeaways From Chapter 8

- If you're going to run ads, spend at least $1000 per month to get an adequate return on investment.
- CTR (click through rate), CPC (cost per click), and conversions are all metrics used to understand how your ads are performing.
- The two main components of advertising online are ad copy and target. These two must be in balance with one another. The ad copy must make sense for the target audience.
- Search ads are ads that show up on search result pages like Google and Bing.
- Display ads are ads that are shown to users as they browse the internet in various places on the internet including websites, email, and Youtube.
- Video ads should have a strong hook to stop the scroll or keep people watching.
- LSA ads are Google Ads using the pay per lead model instead of pay per click. They are not yet available for flight schools.
- Lead generation ads are ads that take user data from within the platform.
- Do not boost posts or use simple mode. Dial in the settings you need. The ad platforms will spend your money unwisely if you do not configure the settings.
- Track and measure your progress constantly.

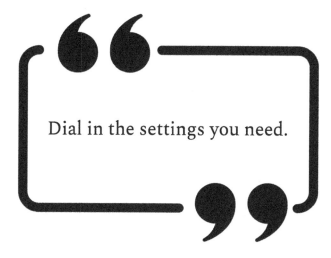

> Dial in the settings you need.

Track Progress and Automate Tasks

Chapter 9

In this chapter we're going to take a look at how to measure your progress. This is important because implementing the Flight School Marketing System at your school is going to take time to see results. So we need to track our progress month after month to ensure that we're staying on track and hitting our goals. Inevitably, growth is not linear. It comes in ups and downs. By keeping an eye out and tracking the performance of our marketing efforts, we can start to think about how to increase our return on investment.

For many of our flight schools, we use a software tool called the Flight School CRM (FSCRM) to measure progress, intake customer data, and send messages. CRM stands for customer relationship management software. A CRM is a database and program that houses information on all of your leads, potential students, and current customers. CRM also provides tools to reach out to and respond to these people so you can create and grow a community around your flight school.

There are many other tools out there that perform similarly to FSCRM like Hubspot, Salesforce, and Monday. It's important to not get caught up in the software, but instead to focus on how to use the tools effectively. Most CRM platforms provide the same functionality, so we can just choose one that makes the most sense for your business and learn how to make the most of it. There is usually a documentation page or a help/support section that outlines the specific procedures you need to follow to make the most of your CRM platform. In this chapter, I'll share how we use FSCRM as that is the software we use for our flight schools, but these concepts can be implemented on all the different CRM platforms.

Figure 9-1. Example of a KPI dashboard in Flight School CRM

We'll first look at key metrics or KPIs (key performance indicators) that will monitor the health of your Flight School Marketing System.

Key Metrics

The expression of "what you focus on expands" is our guiding principle as to why we track certain KPIs. If we pay attention to certain aspects of our business, we can influence them in a positive way. There are primarily two types of KPIs we can think about when it comes to our Flight School Marketing System: Leading and Lagging KPIs.

Leading KPIs refer to metrics that will give you early signs of how well your marketing efforts are doing. These might include things like the number of inquiries you receive each week, the amount of traffic coming to your website, or how many people are clicking on your ads. These metrics help you visualize if you're on the right track before you get the final results.

On the other hand, lagging KPIs show you the outcomes of your marketing activities. These are things like the number of new students who enroll, the revenue generated from those enrollments, and your overall return on investment (ROI). Lagging KPIs are important because they tell you if your efforts are actually paying off, but they only show up after the fact.

Leading KPIs

These KPIs are the easiest to track because most marketing platforms provide these KPIs directly.

- **Website Traffic** - This is easily tracked by adding Google Analytics to your website. When you sign up for a Google Analytics account, you will be provided a code to add to your website. This code will be able to see when people visit your website, where they came

from, and what they do on your website. You can see what pages were most popular and what demographic of visitors are coming to your website.
- ✈ **Ad Conversions** - We went over some other KPIs in *Chapter 8* for ads like CPC and CTR. But the main KPI in regards to PPC advertising is conversions. How many people are clicking on our ads and then submitting information to us or calling us. This is because ad conversions are also leads.
- ✈ **Number of Leads** - This is the number of total people, ads included, that reached out for flight training services. This can be measured in phone calls, form submittals, and walk-ins.
- ✈ **Cost per lead** - This is found by dividing the total money you spent on marketing and dividing the number of total leads.

What you focus on expands

There are other metrics we take into consideration, but I found that these four are the most telling of how well the Flight School Marketing System is working. Other metrics our flight schools find interesting include keyword ranking, heat maps, number of backlinks, most popular pages, CPC, and CTR.

Lagging KPIs

These KPIs focus on the end results of your marketing efforts. They show the actual number of students who enroll and the revenue your flight school generates. Tracking these metrics is important, because they directly measure the effectiveness of your marketing strategies and hence impact on your business's profitability.

- **Enrolled Students** - This metric shows how many new students have signed up as a result of your marketing campaigns.
- **Revenue** - This KPI measures the total income generated from your enrolled students.
- **Cost of Acquisition** - This tracks how much you're spending to acquire each new student. Simply take your marketing costs in a given month and divide that by the number of new students in that month.

Lagging KPIs are the easiest to track. As your business grows and becomes more efficient, you can start looking at more complex KPIs. The following are additional lagging KPIs that we found flight school business owners care about the most, but they are challenging to measure month after month.

- **Student Retention Rate** - This measures how many students continue their training at your school rather than dropping out. High retention indicates satisfaction and effectiveness in your programs.

- **Graduation Rate** - This KPI tracks the percentage of students who successfully complete their training and earn their pilot licenses. A high graduation rate reflects well on your school's ability to guide students to their goals.
- **LTV (Lifetime Value)** - This is the total revenue you can expect from a single customer over the duration of their relationship with your flight school.

Profitability

The final KPI we'll go over isn't directly tied to marketing, but it's the most critical indicator for any business: profitability. It tells you how well your business is truly performing, beyond just the surface numbers. While revenue can give you an idea of how much money is coming in, it doesn't tell the whole story. Profitability shows how much of that revenue is actually being retained after all expenses are paid. As the saying goes, "revenue is vanity, profit is sanity." In other words, it's not just about how much you earn, but how much you keep. Tracking profitability helps ensure that your flight school isn't just generating income, but is also sustainable and growing in the long run.

You'd much rather be responsible for a business that generates $500K in revenue and keeps $150K than a business that generates $1M and keeps the same $150K. A larger revenue means more customers which will in turn mean more headaches and stress.

Another aspect to consider is your involvement in the business. The more entangled you are in the day to day operations, the less freedom you have, and the harder it becomes to scale or even sell the business. If your flight school relies heavily on your presence and decision making, it's not just a business, it's a job. The goal should be to build a business that can run smoothly without you, giving you the option to step back, focus on growth, or explore other ventures.

When your flight school is less dependent on you, it also becomes more attractive to potential buyers. A business that can operate independently is more valuable, because it offers continuity and stability. Buyers are not just purchasing your current revenue, instead they are buying a system that works.

If the business can't run without you, it might be difficult to sell or might require a lengthy and complicated transition period. In the end, a profitable, self-sustaining business is not only more enjoyable to own but also easier to sell when the time comes. Whether you're thinking about selling in the near future or simply want to ensure long term success, focus your efforts on profitability and minimizing your direct involvement.

Industry Averages

You might be asking yourself what are some good numbers for these stats. The answer is that it varies as it depends on the size of your business. The following is an overgeneralization, but it should paint a picture of what to expect and what I see in the flight training market. It can also vary depending if you focus solely on zero to hero programs or run a more traditional ala carte model where students might just do their private or finish up their commercial.

- **Below $500K Annual Revenue**
    - Has around 1-4 aircraft
    - Less than 100 students annually
    - $500-$1000 to acquire a student
- **$500K-$1M Annual Revenue**

- Has around 4-7 aircraft
- 50-150 students annually
- $400-$800 to acquire a student

→ **$1M-$3M Annual Revenue**
- Has around 7-15 aircraft
- 150-300 students annually
- $300-$600 to acquire a student

→ **$3M-$5M Annual Revenue**
- Has around 15-20 aircraft
- 250-500 students annually
- $200-$500 to acquire a student

→ **Above $5M Annual Revenue**
- Has around 20-25+ aircraft
- 300-600+ students annually
- $150-$400 to acquire a student

Most flight schools we see top out below $10M in annual revenue. At this size of a business and maybe even around the $5M range, we are now looking at multiple locations and possibly in multiple states. Considering a LTV of a student to be around $10K, then having an eight figure flight school entails enrolling around 1000 students. Most airports and flight schools can handle around 100 to 300 students in a given month, so horizontally scaling to new locations is the next step. These numbers will vary depending on geographic location and size of airport.

Another thing to note is that as a flight school scales and generates more revenue, the cost to acquire a student goes down and the marketing budget is also not as significant compared to when first starting up. We'll get into how much you should be spending in Chapter 10 where we go over and summarize the steps it takes to implement the Flight School Marketing System at your flight school.

Measuring Steps in Your Sales Process

The next thing we'll go over is measuring the steps in your sales process. As more leads come in through your funnels and lead magnets you installed (Chapter 3), you're going to need a way to track all of this.

We recommend creating a pipeline which outlines the specific steps from inbound leads to enrolled students. Flight School CRM has a feature where you can see in a bird's eye view where the leads are in the sales process. Most flight schools' sales processes go something like this:

- **Inbound lead** - The are leads that contact you after visiting your website and social media. You want to have leads stay in this stage for as short a time as possible, because you should be immediately contacting them when they show interest. Faster reach-outs leads to higher conversions.
- **Contacted** - This is the stage where you or your team reaches out to the prospect and invites them to complete a discovery flight or visit your school. The primary objective for all leads coming in is to get them in the door physically.
- **School Visit** - This is where the lead physically comes to your school and completes a discovery flight or tours your school to meet the team and their potential CFI.
- **Follow Up** - Hopefully after visiting your school they should immediately enroll, but some it may take additional follow up and nurturing.
- **Enrolled Student** - This is the end goal.

I recommend revisiting Chapter 7 and look at Figure 7-1. It shows a bit more detail on the outreach you should be performing at each step of the sales process. Last thing to remember is that your KPI numbers need to be reviewed consistently and frequently. I typically recommend starting out once a month. You should have goals and targets to reach certain KPI numbers in certain timeframes (i.e. weekly, monthly, quarterly, and annually).

In large manufacturing factories where I used to work before getting involved in the aviation industry, me and the team would meet daily and go over production KPI numbers, then review costs and production output. Weekly, we'd go over challenges and issues and look for improvements. Monthly, we'd go over the KPIs in a more bird's eye view perspective. And quarterly and at the end of the year, we'd review the numbers as well.

In regards to your flight school, just make sure to review the KPI numbers consistently, make adjustments, and then refine our processes to get better. Use your CRM as a tool to receive your raw data and help you create your very own KPI reports. Hopefully by using a CRM, you'll be better equipped to make better business decisions and grow your flight school to train more pilots.

Automating Processes

The next part of this chapter is going to go over using your CRM software to automate processes. Part of what we outlined in Figure 7-1 was sending automatic emails and texts depending on certain stages of your sales process. We're going to go over some specific steps to implement this process using Flight School CRM, but these principles can be applied to other CRM software.

Automating some of these processes will help alleviate the workload of your administrative and sales teams which will help your business save time and money.

The foundation of setting up any automation is to define certain trigger events which will initialize an automation workflow. Depending on what you're trying to automate, these triggers will occur when a lead moves from one stage of your pipeline to another stage. Sticking to our example from Chapter 7 which was a discovery flight booking, let's look at what automation and triggers might look like.

The moment someone books an introductory flight at your school, they should receive an automatic email confirmation. This helps validate the process and ensures the prospect that you received the request. How you create the trigger will depend on how you have the form setup on your website to intake discovery flights. In some of our websites, we built an HTML form that sends a POST request to FSCRM. This is also known as a webhook. You can also do similar things with a software called Zapier.

The data is then mapped to a contact and the contact is registered as a lead in our pipeline. From there, FSCRM will send the form submitter an email. In other websites, we build a form using FSCRM and embed that on the website which then directly feeds into the pipeline.

For this stage and this type of automation, even a WordPress plugin like WPForms can do a simple automatic confirmation email. But we'll see as we get more complex and automated, using a CRM tool like FSCRM really comes in handy.

Figure 9-2. Embedded FSCRM Form Trigger

Figure 9-3. FSCRM Webhook Trigger

After the trigger is activated, then we can initiate certain actions like emailing/texting the prospect and also notifying our teams. From there we can place another automation where it sends an email the day of or the day before the scheduled visit.

Below in Figure 9-4 is an example of a pipeline for a flight school where after the contact is added to the CRM, we can track their progress in the sales cycle.

Figure 9-4. Sale pipeline for a flight school with names blurred for privacy

In Figure 9-4, this flight school has it configured to where if a lead is characterized as "won" or an enrolled student, they get moved to another pipeline for onboarding with an enrollment email which outlines specific steps that the new student will need to complete. This includes TSA verification, renter's agreement, and also provides details regarding the syllabus and what to expect.

Figure 9-5. Workflow automation for enrolled students

Figure 9-6. Trigger for enrolled students to activate workflow

This is just a brief overview of how we set up these triggers and then make the CRM send new students an email with the required information. Additional details and procedures for using FSCRM can be found in our documentation site.

https://docs.flightschoolcrm.com

Although these steps only apply to Right Rudder Marketing's FSCRM, the same concepts can be applied to whatever CRM you choose to use.

The important thing to remember is to not rely completely on automation and consider that it is only a tool in your entire marketing repertoire. Don't get caught up in using the newest tool or software. Nothing beats excellent customer service.

Your CRM

In this chapter, we went over the importance of KPIs and also utilizing automation. The reason I combined these two topics is that it's reliant on using a CRM. Choose a CRM that fits your business and start tracking those KPIs to grow your flight school and create automations to save administrative costs and labor. Meet with your team regularly to review your KPIs and strategize ways to improve your business and get better KPI numbers. This is important. Like I mentioned earlier, "what you focus on expands" so you're going to want to keep these numbers visible and public to your team. Having these numbers on display also helps drive home accountability for all team members. It also gives insight to your team as far as how well the business is performing. Use your CRM to generate the numbers and automate processes.

Below is a quick summary of our recommended usage of using a CRM to drive increased sales and better business decisions.

Checklist on How to Use Your CRM

- **Centralize your customer data** - Import data from website forms. When you get phone calls and walk-ins, make sure you document them and add the lead to your CRM.
- **Track Your Leads** - Build out a pipeline and explicitly line out the stages of your sales process. Update the leads in the CRM as they progress through the sales process.
- **Build Out Automations** - Create workflow triggers to send your prospects emails or texts when they reach certain points in the sales process.
- **Track Your Numbers** - Take the numbers from your CRM and track KPIs that drive business growth. Meet with your team members regularly and consistently to review the numbers.

Key Takeaways From Chapter 9

- Leading KPIs refer to metrics that will give you early signs of how well your marketing efforts are doing.
- These KPIs focus on the end results of your marketing efforts.
- Revenue is vanity. Profit is sanity.
- Create a pipeline which outlines the specific steps from inbound leads to enrolled students.
- Focus your efforts on profitability and minimizing your direct involvement in the business.
- Automating processes will help alleviate the workload of your administrative and sales teams which will help your business save time and money.
- Don't get caught up in using the newest tool or software. Nothing beats excellent customer service.
- FSCRM is a free CRM tool given to Right Rudder Marketing flight schools.
- Review the numbers consistently. Meet and share these numbers with your team.

> Review the numbers consistently. Meet and share these numbers with your team.

Create Your Flight School Marketing System

Chapter 10

The previous chapters have all been about implementing the Flight School Marketing System (FSMS) at your flight school. It's a lot of content and material to digest. I remember during my private pilot checkride, the DPE commented before we started the exam that aviation is like drinking out of a firehouse. Marketing? Same thing. It's easy to get lost in the sea of information.

The next few pages are going to be about the specific steps I'm going to recommend you take to launch your next marketing campaign and implement the FSMS framework.

Messaging

We're going to bring it back to the basics that we glossed over in Chapter 2 and walk through the 3Ms again with a new lens. First, define your message and clarify your mission and vision. It's important to not skip over the basics and get this part done first. Define what you want to see your business do. Clarify your company ethos and reset your expectations to your team. Everyone in your organization has a part when it comes to marketing.

You or your administrative staff is going to be responsible for reaching out to your leads and getting them in the door for introductory flights. Your maintenance team is responsible for keeping a clean and presentable hangar and being friendly to aviation newcomers. You and your CFIs will need to be responsible for closing the sale after the prospect's intro flight.

You all need to be beating the same drum, rowing the boat in the same direction, and following the procedures that you as the business owner defines.

Market

Next, you're going to clarify who your correct target customer is and create an experience specifically tailored to that customer. Whether that's block pricing for the low end customer trying to save, or a full scale zero to hero program for folks looking to change careers; figure out an offer that entices your target market.

If your target customers are affluent doctors, business owners, or lawyers, then make sure to create an experience that aligns with their expectations. Fly nicer planes and have a well decorated office and learning areas. If your target customers are of the younger generation, then maybe you need to structure your flight school to mirror traditional educational institutions. Think batch/class dates, group ground school sessions, a game room for relaxation and hanging out.

Whomever you're trying to sell to, make your business fit their needs and expectations and create an experience and a community that they'll choose to stay at.

This is important because when we choose to run our PPC campaigns, we'll have a better idea of how to dial in our settings and show our ads to our target customers which will help us save money.

Medium

Lastly, we need to finally tell the world about our flight school. The first step is updating your website to showcase your new message to your target audience. Make sure you put the relevant keywords into the headers and titles. Embed the keywords within your messaging. Follow the techniques outlined in Chapter 4 and 5. List your business in all the available online directories and make sure your social media is up to date and post frequently.

Run PPC campaigns on Google and Facebook/Instagram. Lock in who you want to target and the keywords you want to appear in.

Then as the leads gradually come into your CRM, implement an email marketing plan. Use the CRM to automate parts of this and lastly, track your data and measure your KPIs.

Just Do It

It might sound easy to implement these strategies, but maintaining consistency day after day, month after month, is challenging to say the least. Some schools run random ad campaigns and quit when they don't see immediate results.

Others spend tens of thousands of dollars redesigning their website, only to find nothing really changes.

The reality is that marketing is complex. It's not a one time task but a continuous process that requires ongoing effort and adjustment. As pilots, we're used to tackling challenges head on, and it's tempting to think that if we can master flying, we can handle growing a business. But running a successful business requires a different set of skills.

Many school owners, or the people they hire, aren't marketing experts. They try to figure it all out on their own, skipping essential steps or lacking the commitment to continually learn and adapt. But marketing and sales is an essential component when it comes to growing a business and we need to continually keep learning and adapting to new trends and changes in the algorithms.

Patience and consistency are key. While ads can spark interest in your flight school, it takes time, often six to twelve months, to see real changes in search rankings and authority. Building a successful flight school is a marathon, not a sprint. It's not a lap around the pattern. It's a long cross country that requires planning and frequent adjustments.

Marketing is a long term investment. For those who haven't yet seen the benefits, the ROI might seem elusive. But marketing is essential to sustaining and growing your business. Without consistent revenue and cash flow, even the best flight schools will struggle to survive.

We didn't start our businesses just to break even. We did it to make an impact and achieve financial freedom. My goal is to help you reach that, but it requires a willingness to invest in marketing.

By implementing the Flight School Marketing System, you now have the tools and knowledge to reduce risk and focus on what actually works. I've seen first hand how owning a multi-million dollar flight school business can transform an owner's life. They are less stressed, more happy, and enjoy greater freedom. I want you to have that.

How Much Does It Cost?

Now that we know marketing is essential, let's discuss costs because flight school owners get caught up on this all the time. A good rule of thumb is to allocate 5% to 10% of your target revenue to marketing. If you aim to generate $1 million in revenue, that means investing $50k to $100k in marketing.

If you choose to run ads and create content yourself, you might spend anywhere from $12k to $60k. But consider the time you're putting in. If you're running a multi-million dollar business, is managing ad campaigns and writing blog posts the best use of your time? Your time is your most valuable asset, and the opportunity cost of doing it all yourself could far exceed $60k when you factor in the sweat equity you'll be putting in.

Building an in-house marketing team can be even more expensive. Salaries, benefits, taxes, plus ad spend and tools, can easily push costs into the six-figure range, especially as your team grows.

Outsourcing to a team of freelancers or a marketing agency can be more cost effective. But you need to ensure you're working with the right people. Does your agency understand the flight training industry? Are they implementing the correct strategies for your Flight School Marketing System?

Right Rudder Marketing

Right Rudder Marketing is different from other marketing agencies and freelancers you may find online. We specialize in the flight training industry because we're pilots too. We know the nuances of Part 61 vs. Part 141 and FAA regulations so you won't waste time explaining the basics and giving free ground lessons.

By partnering with us, you can avoid the costs and headaches of building an in-house marketing department. You don't have to worry about salaries, benefits, or career progression for a marketing team. We handle all of that for you, providing a team of experts dedicated to your flight school's success.

If you're ready to take your flight school to the next level, I encourage you to reach out. Let's work together to train the next generation of aviators and ensure your flight school grows and scales. Give us a call and schedule a time to meet with me or one of my team members. We're here to help you succeed. Let's get to work and train more pilots.

-Tim Jedrek

1-314-804-1200
info@rightruddermarketing.com
https://rightruddermarketing.com/schedule-call

P.S. I hope you found this book insightful. If you have found any benefit from reading this book, I ask that you share this book with a friend and also leave me a 5 star review on Amazon. Your review will help other flight school owners that are in similar situations as yourself.

> Remember why you even started a flight school business in the first place... Let's train the next generation of aviation professionals.

References

1 - https://siteefy.com/how-many-ads-do-we-see-a-day/
2 - http://thefirstbannerad.com/
3 - https://datareportal.com/essential-facebook-stats
4- https://www.statista.com/statistics/324267/us-adults-daily-facebook-minutes/
5, 6 - https://thesocialshepherd.com/blog/facebook-statistics
7 - https://www.tubics.com/blog/youtube-2nd-biggest-search-engine
8 - Youtube Secrets Updated Second Edition Sean Cannell & Benji Travis page 21
9 - FAA Airman Statistics https://www.faa.gov/data_research/aviation_data_statistics/civil_airmen_statistics
10 - https://www.avweb.com/aviation-news/southwest-airlines-scales-back-pilot-hiring-in-2024/
11 - Gunnery, S. D., & Ruben, M. A. (2015). Perceptions of Duchenne and non-Duchenne smiles: A meta-analysis. Cognition and Emotion, 30(3), 501–515. https://doi.org/10.1080/02699931.2015.1018817
12 - Boeing Pilot and Technician Outlook 2023-2042 https://www.boeing.com/commercial/market/pilot-technician-outlook
13 - https://www.semrush.com/goodcontent/content-marketing-blog/copywriting/
14 - https://developers.google.com/search/blog/2018/03/rolling-out-mobile-first-indexing
15 - https://mangools.com/blog/long-tail-keywords/
16 - https://mikekhorev.com/seo-ranking-factors
17 - https://www.wordstream.com/ppc-benchmarks
18 - http://www.iterature.com/adwords/
19 - https://gs.statcounter.com/search-engine-market-share/all/united-states-of-america

Additional Resources

While this book is primarily focused on building your Flight School Marketing System, I figured it'd be a good idea to also include a small section of additional resources that flight schools can use to grow their schools. Throughout the years of running Right Rudder Marketing, I've had the great opportunity to network with other aviation professionals. In addition, we've tried and tested various software tools, so I compiled a short list of our preferred tools.

The ultimate goal of this book is to help flight schools train more pilots. I believe that the below listed resources can benefit anyone starting or growing a flight school business.

- **FSANA** (Flight School Association of North America)
    - Category: Association / Community
    - Provides flight schools with industry knowledge to grow their business and stay up to date. Also hosts an annual conference to provide industry knowledge and connections to flight school owners.
    - Contact: Bob Rockmaker

- **NAFI** (National Association of Flight Instructors)
    - Category: Association / Community
    - Provides knowledge and training to become a better flight instructor. Also hosts an annual conference to provide industry knowledge and connections to flight school owners.
    - Contact: Paul Preidecker

- **King Schools**
    - Category: Training Software
    - Provides ground school training to students. Also hosts an annual conference to provide industry knowledge and connections to flight school owners.
    - Contact: Brian Hough

- **Stratus Financial**
    - Category: Financing company
    - Provides financing to students wishing to complete flight training. Also hosts an annual conference to provide industry knowledge and connections to flight school owners.
    - Contact: Brandon Martini

- **Flight Schools 4 Sale**
    - Category: Business broker and consultant
    - Offers consulting and brokering services for flight schools.
    - Contact: Ari Prevalla

- **Wings Leasing**
    - Category: Leasing company
    - Provides leaseback programs for flight schools to grow their fleet.
    - Contact: Alan Goodnight

- **Milivate**
    - Category: Staffing
    - Implements SkillBridge programs for flight schools looking to grow their teams.
    - Contact: Justin Dal Colletto

- **Four Forces**
    - Category: Flight scheduling
    - Provides a different take on flight school scheduling software. They are continuously listening to customer feedback and upgrading their software.
    - Contact: Brett Hart

- **Plane English**
    - Category: Training software
    - Provides training on radio communication for student pilots.
    - Contact: Muharrem Mane

- **Right Rudder Marketing**
    - Category: Marketing agency
    - Provides marketing services to flight schools to grow their flight school and train more pilots.
    - Contact: Tim Jedrek

- **FSCRM**
    - Category: CRM and analytics
    - Provides software tools to track leads, automate messages, and review KPIs.
    - Contact: Charles Ferguson

- **Google Analytics**
    - Category: Analytics
    - Provides insightful reports to look at user demographics and actions.

- **Search Atlas**
  - Category: Analytics
  - Provides SEO data and website audits.

- **Google Lighthouse** (pagespeed.web.dev)
  - Category: Analytics
  - Provides SEO data and website audits.

- **CallRail**
  - Category: Analytics
  - Swaps phone numbers to trackable numbers to provide insightful reports on incoming calls.

- **Netlify**
  - Category: Web Hosting
  - Our preferred web hosting provider. Allows us to deploy our websites and applications straight from GitHub.

- **ClickCease**
  - Category: Google Ads tools
  - Helps stop robot spam, competitors, and disgruntled customers/employees from wasting Google Ad spend.

- **CloudFlare**
  - Category: Security
  - Creates firewalls and adds security measures to prevent and stop DDOS attacks.

- **Canva**
  - Category: Design tools
  - Easy to use design software to create graphic images for marketing assets.

Testimonials and Reviews

Tim and his team at Right Rudder Marketing are such a great find for aviation companies in need of a professional touch to their marketing portfolio. In my 24 years of experience at Cirrus Aviation Flight Training, it has always been so difficult to find and retain someone with creative abilities that understands aviation, and consistently produces results. Right Rudder understands the industry, produces context-correct content with tracked results, all with a smile.

It is a breath of fresh air to find a professional organization that has experience in the field and provides the services to make it easy to market the image that your organization desires. The guidance and insight that Right Rudder Marketing brings is beyond just a website designer, or communications manager. I have appreciated the perspective brought to the table, and I highly recommend this company. Thanks guys!!!!

★★★★★
Nayda Cattin, Cirrus Aviation
Sarasota, Florida

Amazing Service. Tim and Tonie are the most professional individuals I have ever conducted business with.

★★★★★
Cristopher Freilich, Sun City Aviation Academy
Miami, Florida

The company I work for has been working with Right Rudder Marketing for a while now and I can tell you they have helped us a lot! Our website improved and we started getting more and more inquiries. If you have a flight school you definitely have to work with them!

★★★★★
Mafer Caceres, Sun City Aviation Academy
Miami, Florida

Our flight school has been working with Right Rudder Marketing for almost a year now. They are an incredible group of people. We are so happy with them. Absolutely 100% if you have a flight school and need to work with them!

★★★★★
Marisa Doerstling, Pitcairn Flight Academy
Pottstown, Pennsylvania

Working with Tim and the Right Rudder Marketing team has been a pleasure. Trusting the expertise of Right Rudder Marketing has saved me from the costly mistakes of engaging a marketing agency unfamiliar with the flight training business.

★★★★★
Bill Heckathorn, Ignite Flight Academy
Lincoln, Nebraska

We have been using Right Rudder Marketing for the past 6 months and could not be happier! They revamped our website to make it more user friendly, make consistent updates, and are very responsive to our needs. We have seen a steady increase in web traffic as well as website driven phone calls since starting with Right Rudder Marketing. I can not say enough good things about them!

Kim Nagel, Ideal Aviation
St. Louis, MIssouri

At Red Arrow Flight Academy, we have had an exceptional experience working with Right Rudder Marketing. They completely transformed our website, enhancing its usability and enriching it with valuable content that effectively helps us capture new potential customers. The Right Rudder Marketing team is consistently proactive, not only in maintaining our site but also in seeking innovative ways to support our business. They excel at turning our ideas into reality and are genuinely wonderful to collaborate with. A key aspect we particularly appreciate is their expertise in aviation and flight school marketing, which was a crucial need we were missing when in search for marketing help. If you're searching for a marketing team that provides outstanding results and stellar customer service, Right Rudder Marketing is the perfect choice.

Vanessa Martinez, Red Arrow Flight Academy
Santa Teresa, New Mexico

Made in the USA
Middletown, DE
17 September 2024